STREET HEALING

THOMAS FRANCIS FISCHER

ISBN: 0991177916
ISBN-13:978-0991177912

DEDICATION

This book is dedicated to my dear wife Ahava Sarah Fischer. I'm very grateful to our Lord Jesus Christ for you because you have loved Jesus, His word, me, my family and my friends.

Your passion for excellence is encouraging. You help me stay on course. I'm grateful for all we've been through and excited about all we will experience in the future as we work together to advance the kingdom of God on the earth.

There will be challenges, but we will overcome all of them through Christ our Lord. There will be encouraging times of advancement in the Lord that will spur us on and give us new vision.

There will be new brothers and sisters in the Lord that we'll meet and I pray we have the wisdom to know how to communicate with them and help them in whatever way the Lord would desire. We will have fun times of relaxation in various places that we desire to visit.

We will do all this together as a husband and wife team, just as you have helped me always, including this long awaited book about street healing. Thank you Ahava. I love you.

Your devoted husband Tom.

CONTENTS

	FOREWORD	Pg 1
	INTRODUCTION	Pg 4
1	The years before healing	Pg 10
2	Baptism, Gift or Authority ?	Pg 26
3	The Power and Fire of God	Pg 50
4	The YouTube Videos	Pg 62
5	Unique manifestations	Pg 80
6	The Role of Forgiveness	Pg 88
7	When pain comes back	Pg 101
8	Demons	Pg 111
9	Dreams and Visions	Pg 122
10	Tips on how to minister	Pg 137
11	Cardboard Box Church	Pg 155
12	How I train believers	Pg 161

FOREWORD

FISCHER'S OF MEN

Did you know that God uses social media? YouTube is one of His many ways of reaching the lost.

Nearly three years ago I was sitting on my sofa in my home just outside of Inverness, Scotland, with tears running down my cheeks. I lost my father to cancer in November 2012 and then the following year a good friend. This left me wondering about what happens to us when we die. Even though I didn't know Him yet, the Lord took me on a journey of discovery from seeing demonic things to discovering biblical artifacts and eventually, being led to Jesus Christ - through Tom Fischer and YouTube!

Tom's video "MUST WATCH DRAMATIC NEW YORK HEALING AND SALVATION" was on the side of my screen under recommended videos. I had just watched a video clip of a well known healing minister, where this young girl gets out of a wheelchair and starts dancing and running around to a huge crowd of people. There was music, lights and it all looked a bit fake to me.

I laughed and said to myself, "I wonder how much they paid that girl to do that"?

Then I clicked on Tom's video. Those 15 minutes changed my life. I knew what I was watching was real. There was no need for dramatic music and a light show. I'm sure the young girl getting out of the wheelchair was real, but to me, THIS WAS REAL! The Lord revealed His love for two guys on the video clip and they felt the presence of the Holy Spirit as they got born again on the street. They got healed in such a quick, simple fashion. I was amazed!

I knew in my heart I needed Jesus. He was who I'd been looking for my whole life. After repenting and accepting Jesus as my Lord and Savior, I was completely changed in an instant. The sadness I held in my heart for a year since my Dad died instantly disappeared - Jesus took that away - I felt brand new! I was filled with the Holy Spirit and delivered at the same time.

With a roar, I expelled all of the air in my lungs, but was astonished that a sound kept coming out of me even though all of the air had gone! Wow! Thank you Lord!

I just had to meet Tom and Ahava and get discipled by them, so I invited them over to sunny Scotland (it rained almost every day). The very first miracle I witnessed was in a supermarket on the drive back to our house. A young girl had her arm in a sling and Tom approached her, asked her what happened, quickly prayed for her and left the young lady healed and gobsmacked! I thought to myself "Wow, that was easy"! I wanted to ask her, "Did the pain go? Did it really work?" There was no need to ask because her face said it all!

We had a wonderful week and they baptized us in the sea. Not very clever at any time of the year here, but the sun shone for us! We've been friends with Tom and Ahava Fischer for nearly 3 years now. It's so wonderful to be around this pair.

They ooze Jesus! They both love Him so much. There's not a moment wasted in bringing the Kingdom of God to people wherever they go. On a trip to Disney World in October 2015, we'd often lose sight of one or the other only to see them praying for someone in the distance. What obedient servants!

Their way of preaching the Gospel to people on the streets is brought about in such a way that whoever hears from them, goes away feeling encouraged and amazed. Their ability to teach people and correct them is never done in a condemning way. No one wants to hear that. Preaching hell fire turns people away from hearing anything from you and I just love the warm, friendly way they have with people.

They both work in all the gifts of the Spirit. It's wonderful to see Tom minister healing to someone followed by Ahava prophesying over them in a way that even makes the bystander feel encouraged!

Tom and Ahava recently took the church to the streets, literally, with Cardboard Box Church. What a wonderful idea, a great tool to reach people on the streets and it'll be interesting to see how this develops.

It should be normal Christianity to walk like these guys do. As we go about our daily lives in a humble, loving way, representing Jesus as His ambassadors, signs will follow us. That's what the Word says!

I know that this book will both encourage and build your faith. If you want to know how to walk like a son of God, read this book. If you want to understand how easy it is to heal the sick, read this book. I am eternally grateful to The Lord Jesus Christ and for Him using Tom and Ahava for His glory and in turn, bringing myself and my whole family into the Kingdom. Now let us go to the streets and show the whole world that Jesus is alive!

God Bless the Fischer's and all who read this book.

Tim Curwen

INTRODUCTION

GRACE BE TO YOU, AND PEACE, FROM GOD OUR FATHER, AND FROM THE LORD JESUS CHRIST.

(EPHESIANS 1:2)

Street healing refers to ministering the power and love of God anywhere in the marketplace except, the building called, the church.

The marketplace refers to any location except, the building called, the church. A building is not the church. The body of Christ is the church and the body is made up of many members, all of whom are indispensable. That means that every member of the body is needed to minister the gospel of Jesus Christ in the marketplace.

AND ALL THINGS ARE OF GOD, WHO HATH RECONCILED US TO HIMSELF BY JESUS CHRIST, AND HATH GIVEN TO US THE MINISTRY OF RECONCILIATION; TO WIT, THAT GOD WAS IN CHRIST, RECONCILING THE WORLD UNTO HIMSELF,

NOT IMPUTING THEIR TRESPASSES UNTO THEM;

AND HATH COMMITTED UNTO US THE WORD OF RECONCILIATION.

(2CORINTHIANS 5: 18-19)

Some members of the body do more ministry on the streets than others. That's okay. Our goal is to be available for the Lord Jesus to meet the needs of those around us and not compete with each other. If you're a born-again Christian that means you have the Holy Spirit in you and all the power you will ever need to supernaturally set captives free.

Ministering in the marketplace takes many forms, but healing is the main way I do ministry, so healing will be the focus of this book. I believe that healing is the easiest and quickest way to get the attention of an unbeliever. It often seems as if the ears of an unbeliever pop open after they've experienced the Lord's power and scripture confirms this.

AND THE PEOPLE WITH ONE ACCORD GAVE HEED UNTO THOSE THINGS WHICH PHILIP SPAKE, HEARING AND SEEING THE MIRACLES WHICH HE DID.

(ACTS 8:6)

Of course we want to do more than just get the attention of an unbeliever. We want to disciple unbelievers after they have come to believe the gospel message. This is the part that can be tricky because not everyone who gets healed is going to want to be discipled.

Discipling is another book entirely and there's much to say about the whole process of ministering healing. I hope and pray that what I have to share from my own experience will help you.

After you've read this book, you will gain a greater understanding of the truth of God's word as it pertains to operating in the supernatural power of the Holy Spirit and you will learn to enjoy serving the Lord without striving to please him,

If you have seen the YouTube videos that I have published, you know that I have a lot of fun ministering in the marketplace.

You have to really enjoy what you're doing in order to have fun with it everyday. Ministering healing is lots of fun and very rewarding because I get to see joyful reactions from people being healed. There's nothing more rewarding than watching the joyful reaction of someone being supernaturally touched by the Lord. Perhaps this is the main reason why the people of Israel flocked to Jesus everywhere he went. He spoke and ministered with such great love, compassion and authority that people were even willing to follow him for days without eating. I believe they were so mesmerized by him that they actually forgot to eat. They were enjoying so much spiritual food that they may not have sensed a natural hunger for food.

You can have this joy as you minister the power of God to people in need. I firmly believe in the supernatural power of God and have prayed over this book so that you will be blessed by reading it and implementing the sound, biblical advice found on its pages. Thank you for purchasing this book and thanks for helping my wife Ahava and I to continue doing what we love doing.

I pray,

THAT THE GOD OF OUR LORD JESUS

CHRIST, THE FATHER OF GLORY, MAY GIVE UNTO YOU THE SPIRIT OF WISDOM AND REVELATION IN THE KNOWLEDGE OF HIM:

THE EYES OF YOUR UNDERSTANDING BEING ENLIGHTENED;

THAT YE MAY KNOW WHAT IS THE HOPE OF HIS CALLING,

AND WHAT THE RICHES OF THE GLORY OF HIS INHERITANCE IN THE SAINTS AND WHAT IS THE EXCEEDING GREATNESS OF HIS POWER TO US-WARD WHO BELIEVE,

ACCORDING TO THE WORKING OF HIS MIGHTY POWER, WHICH HE WROUGHT IN CHRIST,

WHEN HE RAISED HIM FROM THE DEAD AND SET HIM AT HIS OWN RIGHT HAND IN THE HEAVENLY PLACES,

FAR ABOVE ALL PRINCIPALITY AND POWER AND MIGHT AND DOMINION AND EVERY NAME THAT IS NAMED,

NOT ONLY IN THIS WORLD,

BUT ALSO IN THAT WHICH IS TO COME:

AND HATH PUT ALL THINGS UNDER HIS FEET AND GAVE HIM TO BE THE HEAD OVER ALL THINGS TO THE CHURCH, WHICH IS HIS BODY, THE FULNESS OF HIM THAT FILLETH ALL IN ALL.

(EPHESIANS 1:17-23)

1
THE YEARS BEFORE HEALING

I grew up in a very busy household with my mom, dad and 5 brothers. Both mom and dad have gone to be with the Lord. All 5 of my brothers are still alive and we all get along with each other.

My mom was always busy doing something. If she wasn't cooking, she was cleaning or doing some other household task. Mom was always in a good mode. She loved to laugh and have a good, good time. If she was with her family that was all that mattered. She was devoted to the Lord, her husband and her children.

Dad taught us how to work hard, but mom taught us love and faith. We all learn from our parents and I recognize in my own life those things I learned from them both.

As I got older I realized the good things I learned and the not so good things.

Concerning the not so good things, I don't blame my parents because they picked up bad things from their parents.

This is the nature of the sinful flesh. As you grow in Jesus, these bad things about the flesh begin to grieve you more and more. It's good that the corrupt nature of the flesh grieves you. It shows you're sensitive to the Holy Spirit and that you don't want to grieve Him. Thank God for Jesus.

Paul the Apostle was also grateful for Jesus concerning this issue of the flesh.

FOR I KNOW THAT IN ME (THAT IS, IN MY FLESH,) DWELLETH NO GOOD THING:

FOR TO WILL IS PRESENT WITH ME; BUT HOW TO PERFORM THAT WHICH IS GOOD I FIND NOT.

FOR THE GOOD THAT I WOULD I DO NOT: BUT THE EVIL WHICH I WOULD NOT, THAT I DO.

NOW IF I DO THAT I WOULD NOT, IT IS NO MORE I THAT DO IT, BUT SIN THAT DWELLETH IN ME.

I FIND THEN A LAW, THAT, WHEN I

WOULD DO GOOD, EVIL IS PRESENT WITH ME.

FOR I DELIGHT IN THE LAW OF GOD AFTER THE INWARD MAN:

BUT I SEE ANOTHER LAW IN MY MEMBERS, WARRING AGAINST THE LAW OF MY MIND, AND BRINGING ME INTO CAPTIVITY TO THE LAW OF SIN WHICH IS IN MY MEMBERS.

O WRETCHED MAN THAT I AM! WHO SHALL DELIVER ME FROM THE BODY OF THIS DEATH?

I THANK GOD THROUGH JESUS CHRIST OUR LORD. SO THEN WITH THE MIND I MYSELF SERVE THE LAW OF GOD; BUT WITH THE FLESH THE LAW OF SIN.

(ROMANS 7:18-25)

I'm not making excuses for sinning because a time is coming when we'll be held accountable for sin if we don't submit to the Lord and turn from it.

THERE IS THEREFORE NOW NO CONDEMNATION TO THEM WHICH ARE IN CHRIST JESUS,

WHO WALK NOT AFTER THE FLESH, BUT AFTER THE SPIRIT.

FOR THE LAW OF THE SPIRIT OF LIFE IN CHRIST JESUS HATH MADE ME FREE FROM THE LAW OF SIN AND DEATH.

(ROMANS 8:1-2)

When I was young I was a fast runner. All the neighborhood kids would play chain tag and I was usually the last one caught. If I like something, I have to do it well.

In grades 4-6 the gym teacher would set up 4 cones out on the grass, each one equally spaced, so that 3 loops around the cones would measure approximately 600 yards in length. I always won.

When I got to high school, I signed up for the cross-country team in the fall and the track team in the spring. I was a decent runner my freshman year, but by the end of my second year, I was one of the best runners in the state.

By the time I graduated high school, I was the best runner in the state and one of the best in America. I made All-American honors for both cross-country and track.

KNOW YE NOT THAT THEY WHICH RUN IN A RACE RUN ALL, BUT ONE RECEIVETH THE PRIZE?

SO RUN, THAT YE MAY OBTAIN. AND EVERY MAN THAT STRIVETH FOR THE MASTERY IS TEMPERATE IN ALL THINGS. NOW THEY DO IT TO OBTAIN A CORRUPTIBLE CROWN; BUT WE AN INCORRUPTIBLE.

I THEREFORE SO RUN, NOT AS UNCERTAINLY; SO FIGHT I, NOT AS ONE THAT BEATETH THE AIR:

BUT I KEEP UNDER MY BODY, AND BRING IT INTO SUBJECTION: LEST THAT BY ANY MEANS, WHEN I HAVE PREACHED TO OTHERS, I MYSELF SHOULD BE A CASTAWAY.

(1CORINTHIANS 9:24-27)

I had friends who helped me to succeed.

Two of them in particular were Tim Anderson and John Casey. It's interesting how our life experiences and friends help prepare us for what we'll do for the Lord once we come to Him and recognize His will for us.

Tim Anderson was a senior in high school when I was a freshman. Tim was a very good runner and I can remember coming home from cross country or track races very excited and telling my parents that Tim had once again, won the race.

Tim won a lot of races because he was committed to his craft and that inspired me. He also showed an interest in me, which was another source of inspiration because seniors, often ignore freshmen.

Those who blaze a trail for others to follow are doing a good thing. Tim and his wife Lori have been good friends for over 38 years.

I lost contact with Tim and Lori for many years when they moved from New Jersey to North Carolina, but Tim sort me out to re-establish our friendship, which I thought was incredibly admirable because it was similar to what Jesus does as He seeks His lost friends.

John Casey ran cross country and track along side me day after day all through high school. A bond is created between friends who experience many different situations together and the result is a friendship that can't be defined with a few words.

As a result of our mutual training together in high school, we've trusted each other over the years in many life and work situations. I believe God made these friendships possible before the world even began. John and his wife Kimberly have been friends for over 38 years. They're a blessing from the Lord.

IRON SHARPENETH IRON; SO A MAN SHARPENETH THE COUNTENANCE OF HIS FRIEND.

(PROVERBS 27:17)

Good coaches are vitally important.

Cordell Reinhardt and Bill Bruno were instrumental in my success. They taught me how to compete with integrity. Both coaches knew how to recognize and draw out the talent in me.

I can remember both coaches telling me of my ability to accomplish certain things that I didn't know I could accomplish. Coaches recognize ability that trainees commonly don't recognize.

WITHOUT COUNSEL PURPOSES ARE DISAPPOINTED: BUT IN THE MULTITUDE OF COUNSELLORS THEY ARE ESTABLISHED.

(PROVERBS 15:22)

By the time I was halfway through college I was turning away from a disciplined life of athletics. I left the path of excellence, even though I gained so much from friends and coaches.

At home I was raised by a God-fearing, loving mom and a hard working dad. Mom loved her six sons unconditionally. Dad loved us as well, but didn't know how to show it because he didn't experience much of it growing up.

We usually said our prayers and went to church on Sunday, but when I turned 18 I stopped going to church. The only time I opened a bible was to look at the pictures.

I remained active and hardworking as I started a lawn maintenance business in the late 80's. In 1991 I stopped cutting grass and started a door to door business selling flash frozen foods, such as steaks, chicken, seafood, etc.

I also tried my luck at the Amway business, which is a multilevel marketing business. I enjoyed the Amway products, but couldn't achieve success with the marketing plan and eventually quit.

However, before I quit, something happened that changed my life forever.

August 19, 1991 was a beautiful, sunny day.

I was living in Freehold, NJ, sharing an apartment with my friend Joel Horowitz.

I needed to have a phone installed so I made plans for a technician to come out to the apartment. The man hadn't been there all that long before I started sharing my spiel about the Amway marketing plan in order to sign him up.

His name was Tom Geoffroy and unbeknownst to me, he wasn't just a telephone technician. Tom Geoffroy was also a minister.

I wasn't quite sure what a minister was, but I knew it had something to do with being some sort of important person in church. As he's listening to my spiel he stops what he's doing and says to me, "You know, you shouldn't love money so much."

I wasn't expecting to hear that, so I replied, "I don't love money. Everyone needs money." He said a few other things and then began to quote the bible to me. At this point I was becoming intrigued because I had never met anyone in society who quoted the bible.

I specifically remember him telling me that I needed to be born-again.

VERILY, VERILY, I SAY UNTO THEE, EXCEPT A MAN BE BORN AGAIN, HE CANNOT SEE THE KINGDOM OF GOD. (JOHN 3:3)

I had no idea what that meant, but I found myself agreeing with it because in the Amway business part of the learning process was listening to cassette tapes of successful business owners and often I would hear one of them say they were born-again. These rich Amway distributors had great attitudes and so I was quick to sign up for this born-again thing.

Tom, the phone technician/minister thinks I'm ready to believe the good news about Jesus, so he further explains the gospel to me and then leads me in a prayer to receive Jesus as my Lord and Savior. I didn't feel any different, but I guess I was excited about being a better person and a better Amway distributor.

It didn't end there because this man did a lot of things right as far as discipling is concerned. After he led me in a prayer to receive Christ into my life, he tells me he lives around the corner and has a pool and would like for me to come over to his home so that he could baptize me in his pool.

For some reason I was saying yes to everything he suggested, so I agreed to be baptized. After he left my apartment, I changed into swim trunks and went over to his home.

When I arrived, he was already in the middle of his above ground pool with a bible in his hand. I noticed his wife standing in the doorway of the sliding glass doors. She waved to me and I waved back and then I got into the pool. Tom shared some scripture verses with me and then down I go to be baptized.

When I came up, he was muttering some sort of gibberish which shocked and confused me. He tells me to open my mouth and do as he's doing as he explains to me about tongues. It's worth noting that I didn't just break out in tongues, but, rather, was encouraged to do as he was doing.

Some believers have a problem with this and I used to be one of them. However, the bible does teach us to open our mouths and God will fill it.

I AM THE LORD THY GOD, WHICH BROUGHT THEE OUT OF THE LAND OF EGYPT: OPEN THY MOUTH WIDE, AND I WILL FILL IT. (PSALM 81:10)

I began to speak in tongues.

Next, he invites me to his church.

If you're a seasoned believer, you know that not every bad habit immediately falls away upon believing in the Lord Jesus Christ.

That Saturday night I went out drinking with some friends and had a bit too much. However, the next day I did go to church because I said I would.

I walk in and Tom is standing at the doorway going into the sanctuary. The first thing out of my mouth was, "Wow, I have such a bad hangover." He looks at me shocked and replies, "You're not suppose to be getting drunk." I replied with the question, "You're not?"

I laugh whenever I think back to that situation. I enjoyed attending the church he introduced me to, which is called "Monmouth Worship Center".

Tom Geoffroy no longer attends this church, but the church still exists and continues to help people. The pastor's name is Ken Jasko. He's a very effective minister for the kingdom. I attended this church for about a year and remember thinking to myself, concerning Ken's preaching, "How does this man know all this stuff about God"?

Years go by and I continue to go to church and read my bible. There were several times when I was backsliding to the point of not attending church, but for some reason I always maintained a desire to read the bible.

I love reading God's word.

Sometimes I wonder if I would have gone to heaven if I died in my backslidden spiritual condition. I know there are many Christians that believe I would've, but there are also many who aren't so sure. I don't know for certain, but it's a scary thought to consider the consequences of backsliding because of the strong words the bible has to say on the topic.

AND JESUS SAID UNTO HIM, NO MAN, HAVING PUT HIS HAND TO THE PLOUGH, AND LOOKING BACK, IS FIT FOR THE KINGDOM OF GOD.

(LUKE 9:62)

EXAMINE YOURSELVES,

WHETHER YE BE IN THE FAITH; PROVE YOUR OWN SELVES.

KNOW YE NOT YOUR OWN SELVES, HOW THAT JESUS CHRIST IS IN YOU,

EXCEPT YE BE REPROBATES?

(2CORINTHIANS 13:5)

There are many other verses that deal with this subject. A word search of the word, backslidden or backsliding in the scriptures will reveal more information.

In the late 90's I experienced supernatural healing for the first time.

I was attending Faith Fellowship Ministries World Outreach Center in Edison, NJ. The pastor was and still is, David Demola, along with his wife Diane the Co-Pastor. One day Pastor Demola announced that there would be a healing service for those who needed healing.

I thought to myself, "How can you schedule a miracle? Isn't that something God decides on His own?"

Nevertheless, I decided to go because I had pain in my right hand that wasn't going away and I didn't have health insurance. Pastor Demola calls people to the front and when he gets to me, he gives my a tap to the forehead with the heel of his hand.

Amazingly, the power of God floods my whole body, goes down my right arm and out my hand taking the pain with it. I was blown away at this.

However, not long after, the pain came back. I remember thinking, "That darn devil stole my healing!"

The next day in church Pastor Demola comments that many people were healed and so there would be another healing service at the Thursday night church service.

"I'm going and I'm getting my healing back", I thought to myself. I go to the front and he does the same thing with the heel of his hand, but this time nothing happens.

He says to me, "Is it gone?" "No," I replied. "Don't worry, it will," he says. I took him at his word and sat back down.

As I was sitting there all the pain left and never came back. I learned an important lesson in all that. The first healing was accompanied by all the warm, fuzzy feelings of God's manifest power flowing through me, but the pain came back. The second healing had no warm, fuzzy feelings, but the healing remained.

The lesson was clear.

The healing was not in the warm, fuzzy feelings.

Sometime around the year 2000 I started to realize that I was called to share the gospel message with others.

Every now and then I would tell people about Jesus and once in awhile I would lead someone to receive Christ. It was always a good feeling to know I helped someone recognize the truth.

I didn't know much about healing, except that Jesus would heal people that needed to be healed, so at times I would pray for those who needed prayer for whatever reason, not really expecting anything to happen immediately.

After a couple years of this I began to develop a desire to experience the power to heal people.

2

BAPTISM, GIFT OR AUTHORITY?

It was late summer of 2008 and I was continually asking the Lord to use me in healing.

ASK, AND IT SHALL BE GIVEN YOU;

SEEK, AND YE SHALL FIND;

KNOCK, AND IT SHALL BE OPENED UNTO YOU.

(MATTHEW 7:7)

Besides asking, I was spending a lot of time worshiping the Lord in my bedroom. If I wasn't learning about healing from Benny Hinn, I was worshiping the Lord in song with lots of good worship music.

Benny Hinn was one of only a few that I was aware of who ministered healing, so I listened to him. Of course there were many others, but Benny seemed to be in the spotlight the most at the time.

One night as I was sleeping, I had an experience that changed everything about the way I ministered. I was sleeping on my stomach with my arms down to my sides and the palms of my hands up in the air. I don't normally sleep like that, but I was exhausted.

All of a sudden, two hands grabbed both my hands simultaneously. I began to see what was happening in my mind's eye. Something like hot putty was pressed down into the palms of both my hands. This shocked me and as I was coming out of sleep I immediately pulled my hands loose and turned over onto my back.

At this point I was experiencing more peace than I had ever experienced before and the palms of my hands were burning hot. I knew the experience was from God because of the peace.

Peace is the gauge in order to know if what your experiencing is from God or the devil.

AND MY PEOPLE SHALL DWELL IN A PEACEABLE HABITATION, AND IN SURE DWELLINGS, AND IN QUIET RESTING PLACES.

(ISAIAH 32:19)

PEACE I LEAVE WITH YOU, MY PEACE I GIVE UNTO YOU: NOT AS THE WORLD GIVETH, GIVE I UNTO YOU. LET NOT YOUR HEART BE TROUBLED, NEITHER LET IT BE AFRAID.

(JOHN 14:27)

I had a strong feeling that two angels had just put that hot putty into my hands. I began to speak to the angels, "Just to make sure that was angels, now do that to my feet, but this time don't hold my feet".

Within 5 or 6 seconds the balls of my feet started getting hot. I'm lying in bed with the palms of my hands and the balls of my feet burning hot and with great peace having filled the room.

God didn't part the heavens and say, "I have given you the gift of healing".

No, I had to figure out for myself what was given to me.

Was I given the gift of healing or was it the baptism of the Holy Spirit? I wrestled with that question for quite some time even though I had already been a born-again Christian for 17 years. I thought I had received the baptism of the Holy Spirit when I got saved and baptized in water because I spoke in tongues. Ever since I've been ministering in healing, I've come to realize that the main evidence of the baptism of the Holy Spirit isn't speaking in different tongues, but power.

BUT YE SHALL RECEIVE POWER,

AFTER THAT THE HOLY GHOST IS COME UPON YOU:

AND YE SHALL BE WITNESSES UNTO ME

BOTH IN JERUSALEM, AND IN ALL JUDAEA, AND IN SAMARIA, AND UNTO THE UTTERMOST PART OF THE EARTH.

(ACTS 1:8)

Tongues was the main sign at the day of Pentecost because there were Jews in Jerusalem from many nations speaking different languages. They were able to understand what the disciples were saying, even though the disciples had never formally learned their language.

This is why the sign was a tongue of fire above each disciple's head.

AND THERE APPEARED UNTO THEM CLOVEN TONGUES LIKE AS OF FIRE, AND IT SAT UPON EACH OF THEM. (ACTS 2:3)

I'm not saying I didn't receive the baptism of the Holy Spirit when I believed and was baptized in water. I believe I did, but the evidence of power wasn't there because I wasn't fully taught about my identity in Christ after having believed. This isn't an indictment on any of my teachers at the time, but it's important that we teach new believers that they have supernatural power in them once they receive the Holy Spirit.

BUT THE MANIFESTATION OF THE SPIRIT IS GIVEN TO EVERY MAN TO PROFIT WITHAL.

(1CORINTHIANS 12:7)

If you're born-again you have supernatural power in you that needs to be released to a lost and dying world.

I eventually came to believe that I received the gift of healing.

BUT THE MANIFESTATION OF THE SPIRIT IS GIVEN TO EVERY MAN TO PROFIT WITHAL.

FOR TO ONE IS GIVEN BY THE SPIRIT THE WORD OF WISDOM;

TO ANOTHER THE WORD OF KNOWLEDGE BY THE SAME SPIRIT; TO ANOTHER FAITH

BY THE SAME SPIRIT;

TO ANOTHER THE GIFTS OF HEALING BY THE SAME SPIRIT;

TO ANOTHER THE WORKING OF MIRACLES;

TO ANOTHER PROPHECY;

TO ANOTHER DISCERNING OF SPIRITS;

TO ANOTHER DIVERS KINDS OF TONGUES;

TO ANOTHER THE INTERPRETATION OF TONGUES:

BUT ALL THESE WORKETH THAT ONE AND THE SELFSAME SPIRIT, DIVIDING TO EVERY MAN SEVERALLY AS HE WILL.

(1CORINTHIANS 12:7-11)

So, in other words, I received the baptism of the Holy Spirit when I became a born-again Christian on August 19, 1991 and then received the gift of healing on the night of this amazing experience 17 years later. Some may chose to believe that gifts are given at conversion and that may be true. If it is, then I can at least say that something was activated on that night 17 years after conversion.

There's clearly a misunderstanding in the body of Christ concerning the gift of healing and the authority all believers have in Christ.

Having the gift of healing doesn't mean I can heal anyone or everyone at will.

The gift is something that stirs up in me when the Lord wills to heal someone. The Lord will use me based on the situations He planned in advance and in accordance with the measure of faith I operate in with the gift.

Having just written this, I'm reminded of a healing situation that occurred last night when Ahava and I met friends for dinner. Mark and Debbie Searcy had recently returned from Panama. They took a trip there because they have plans to minister in Panama in the near future.

Ahava and I arrived at the restaurant before them and sat down at a table. When they arrived, we greeted them with a hug. As I was hugging Debbie, I felt the power of God. Twenty minutes later, I felt the power of God again for her. I asked her where the pain was and she said in her feet.

With my hands open towards her feet, I released the power I knew the Lord wanted to be released and she felt tingling in her feet. Five minutes later she mentioned how good her feet felt.

The next day she called Ahava and told us that her feet hadn't felt that good since they returned from Panama 2 weeks ago. Apparently she picked up some attack from the enemy while in Panama. She's a faithful servant of the Lord, so the victory was hers.

That situation was the gift in action. I didn't know it was going to happen. The power just surged through my hands and I knew it was for Debbie. When a believer recognizes the gift in them, all that believer has to do is walk with the Lord in obedience to His word and be available whenever the Lord wants to move in power.

This is the leading of the Spirit and it makes ministry effortless.

FOR I SAY, THROUGH THE GRACE GIVEN UNTO ME, TO EVERY MAN THAT IS AMONG YOU, NOT TO THINK OF HIMSELF MORE HIGHLY THAN HE OUGHT TO THINK;

BUT TO THINK SOBERLY, ACCORDING AS GOD HATH DEALT TO EVERY MAN THE MEASURE OF FAITH. FOR AS WE HAVE

MANY MEMBERS IN ONE BODY, AND ALL MEMBERS HAVE NOT THE SAME OFFICE:

SO WE, BEING MANY, ARE ONE BODY IN CHRIST, AND EVERY ONE MEMBERS ONE OF ANOTHER. HAVING THEN GIFTS DIFFERING ACCORDING TO THE GRACE THAT IS GIVEN TO US,

WHETHER PROPHECY, LET US PROPHESY ACCORDING TO THE PROPORTION OF FAITH;

OR MINISTRY, LET US WAIT ON OUR MINISTERING:

OR HE THAT TEACHETH, ON TEACHING; OR HE THAT EXHORTETH, ON EXHORTATION: HE THAT GIVETH, LET HIM DO IT WITH SIMPLICITY;

HE THAT RULETH, WITH DILIGENCE; HE THAT SHEWETH MERCY, WITH CHEERFULNESS.

(ROMANS 12:3-8)

Some of the words that stand out for me in these scripture verses are, "Not to think more highly of himself than he ought to think."

I have often allowed others to convince me of their way of thinking and this has resulted in confusion.

There are many believers who teach exclusively on the authority of the believer as if there aren't any gifts. Everything we have is a gift, including the boldness to teach on authority. A gifting will not prevent a believer from teaching incorrectly. It seems to me that many believers teach exclusively on authority because it's very popular with those who want to get results operating in the power of the Spirit, but don't feel as if they have the gift of healing.

Knowing your authority in Christ is vital, but you're better off recognizing how the Lord uses you in gifting, because it will eliminate frustration from not getting someone healed because you think the Lord is ready to heal at all times.

Don't get me wrong, the Lord is ready at all times, but He often waits until the person needing healing is ready to receive. Learn to recognize when the Lord is moving in power.

Your life in the Lord will be a delight.

I do believe in teaching on the authority of the believer, but it's important to keep a balance, based on what the whole of scripture teaches. I've already quoted scripture showing the gifts and the use of them in proportion to the faith allotted to each believer and now I will share scripture about authority.

Jesus told his disciples that he had given them authority over the works of the enemy.

BEHOLD, I GIVE UNTO YOU POWER TO TREAD ON SERPENTS AND SCORPIONS, AND OVER ALL THE POWER OF THE ENEMY: AND NOTHING SHALL BY ANY MEANS HURT YOU.

(LUKE 10:19)

Jesus said this in response to what his disciples said when they returned from the mission he sent them on to heal the sick and cast out devils. There's no indication of failure on the part of the disciples with any of the healing and deliverance situations they found themselves involved in.

However, this doesn't negate what the scripture says about operating in the level of faith given to us. Jesus led each of these disciples into situations he had orchestrated. He was training them, so he gave them healing and deliverance situations where they would experience results. You may be thinking, "How do you justify this reasoning Tom"?

We see in scripture where disciples couldn't get the job done and Jesus explains why.

AND WHEN THEY WERE COME TO THE MULTITUDE, THERE CAME TO HIM A CERTAIN MAN, KNEELING DOWN TO HIM, AND SAYING, LORD, HAVE MERCY ON MY SON: FOR HE IS LUNATICK, AND SORE VEXED: FOR OFTTIMES HE FALLETH INTO THE FIRE, AND OFT INTO THE WATER.

AND I BROUGHT HIM TO THY DISCIPLES, AND THEY COULD NOT CURE HIM.

THEN JESUS ANSWERED AND SAID, O FAITHLESS AND PERVERSE GENERATION, HOW LONG SHALL I BE WITH YOU? HOW LONG SHALL I SUFFER YOU? BRING HIM HITHER TO ME.

AND JESUS REBUKED THE DEVIL; AND HE DEPARTED OUT OF HIM: AND THE CHILD WAS CURED FROM THAT VERY HOUR.

THEN CAME THE DISCIPLES TO JESUS APART, AND SAID, WHY COULD NOT WE CAST HIM OUT?

AND JESUS SAID UNTO THEM, BECAUSE OF YOUR UNBELIEF: FOR VERILY I SAY

UNTO YOU, IF YE HAVE FAITH AS A GRAIN OF MUSTARD SEED, YE SHALL SAY UNTO THIS MOUNTAIN, REMOVE HENCE TO YONDER PLACE; AND IT SHALL REMOVE; AND NOTHING SHALL BE IMPOSSIBLE UNTO YOU.

HOWBEIT THIS KIND GOETH NOT OUT BUT BY PRAYER AND FASTING.

(MATTHEW 17:14-21)

When developing a doctrinal understanding, it's important to use the preponderance of scripture, meaning all of scripture. If I make a statement that I want people to believe as being part of a whole doctrinal understanding and someone can show me scripture that opposes what I'm saying, then that person has just cast doubt into what I'm claiming to be doctrine.

The scripture verses in Matthew 17 show how the disciples couldn't cast out a demon, yet Luke 10:19, which I also just quoted, says we have authority over all demons. That's how I justify my reasoning. Authority has to be exercised properly through faith. This puts responsibility on the believer.

The responsibility is prayer and fasting, as is noted in

Matthew 17:21. Many believers don't like the word fasting and to be honest with you, neither do I.

However, it's my flesh that hates it and not the inner man of the Spirit. What Jesus did through the cross empowered the believer to overcome the flesh. When I decide that I'm not going to let my flesh dictate to me what my behavior should be at any given moment, I strengthen my belief in the new creation of the inner man. This results in supernatural peace no matter what my circumstances are.

A believer won't pray and fast effectively unless abiding in peace.

If I'm not seeing the results I think I should be seeing because I've already decided on what I believe is an accurate understanding of my authority, then my thinking is faulty.

Can I get better results with my authority? Of course, but it's not based simply on one scripture that says I have authority at the expense of another scripture that teaches me how to increase my faith in order to effectively use my authority.

Some believers would say this isn't accurate because the disciples who couldn't cast out the demon, weren't born-again. Hence, they didn't have the Holy Spirit living in them yet. I will share why that reasoning isn't accurate and my answer will lead back into the emphasis of the use of a gift.

In Acts 8 Philip goes down to Samaria to preach the gospel and many people are set free from demons and healed of various sicknesses. Philip also baptizes many of them in water. However, when the Apostles Peter and John hear about this, they go to Samaria and recognize that these new believers hadn't received the baptism of the Holy Spirit.

When Peter and John lay their hands on them they get baptized into the Holy Spirit.

BUT WHEN THEY BELIEVED PHILIP PREACHING THE THINGS CONCERNING THE KINGDOM OF GOD, AND THE NAME OF JESUS CHRIST, THEY WERE BAPTIZED, BOTH MEN AND WOMEN.

THEN SIMON HIMSELF BELIEVED ALSO: AND WHEN HE WAS BAPTIZED, HE CONTINUED WITH PHILIP, AND WONDERED, BEHOLDING THE MIRACLES AND SIGNS WHICH WERE DONE.

NOW WHEN THE APOSTLES WHICH WERE AT JERUSALEM HEARD THAT SAMARIA

HAD RECEIVED THE WORD OF GOD, THEY SENT UNTO THEM PETER AND JOHN: WHO, WHEN THEY WERE COME DOWN, PRAYED FOR THEM, THAT THEY MIGHT RECEIVE THE HOLY GHOST:

(FOR AS YET HE WAS FALLEN UPON NONE OF THEM: ONLY THEY WERE BAPTIZED IN THE NAME OF THE LORD JESUS.)

THEN LAID THEY THEIR HANDS ON THEM, AND THEY RECEIVED THE HOLY GHOST.

(ACTS 8:12-17)

The point I'm making is that Philip didn't get them baptized in the Spirit, although he was doing great miracles.

Why is this? The scripture tells us why. Simon the sorcerer, who wasn't even right with God recognized that the Spirit was given by the laying on of the Apostle's hands. Philip wasn't an Apostle. He was a disciple and an evangelist, but not an Apostle.

This puts the emphasis back onto a gift. God assigns some to be this and others to be that. On a side note, it's interesting how the scripture shows us that Simon the Sorcerer wasn't saved, although he believed the message and was baptized in water.

If we try to be something we're not, we will fail. There's order in what God does. This doesn't mean we can't have more of what God has, because the scripture is clear that we can.

AND GOD HATH SET SOME IN THE CHURCH,

FIRST APOSTLES,

SECONDARILY PROPHETS,

THIRDLY TEACHERS,

AFTER THAT MIRACLES,

THEN GIFTS OF HEALINGS,

HELPS, GOVERNMENTS, DIVERSITIES OF TONGUES.

ARE ALL APOSTLES?

ARE ALL PROPHETS?

ARE ALL TEACHERS?

ARE ALL WORKERS OF MIRACLES?

HAVE ALL THE GIFTS OF HEALING?

DO ALL SPEAK WITH TONGUES?

DO ALL INTERPRET?

BUT COVET EARNESTLY THE BEST GIFTS: AND YET SHEW I UNTO YOU A MORE EXCELLENT WAY.

(1CORINTHIANS 12:28-31)

These verses clearly show that believers have different gifts. However, if we eagerly desire more, God will give us more. How do we eagerly desire more? There are spiritual exercises, some of which have just been mentioned, meaning, prayer and fasting. Other things a believer can do to receive more from the Lord include being faithful with what He has already given you.

HE THAT IS FAITHFUL IN THAT WHICH IS LEAST IS FAITHFUL ALSO IN MUCH: AND HE THAT IS UNJUST IN THE LEAST IS UNJUST ALSO IN MUCH.

(LUKE 16:10)

The context of this scripture verse is money, but the point applies to supernatural gifts because that is what Jesus means in verse 11.

IF THEREFORE YE HAVE NOT BEEN

FAITHFUL IN THE UNRIGHTEOUS MAMMON, WHO WILL COMMIT TO YOUR TRUST THE TRUE RICHES?

(LUKE 16:11)

The true riches refers to the power of the Holy Spirit. Christianity is the ministry of the Spirit. It has nothing to do with what we can accomplish on our own strength. If I follow Jesus faithfully and give away what He wants me to give, He will promote me. I can't put a definition on what promotion looks like, but I believe I can say for certain that it comes with honor.

BEFORE DESTRUCTION THE HEART OF MAN IS HAUGHTY, AND BEFORE HONOUR IS HUMILITY.

(PROVERBS 18:12)

THE FEAR OF THE LORD IS THE INSTRUCTION OF WISDOM; AND BEFORE HONOUR IS HUMILITY.

(PROVERBS 15:33)

If I'm walking in humility, the Lord is able to lead me into good things. If I'm proud, I'm heading in the direction of trouble.

I have operated in both the gift of healing and the authority of the believer. In fact, I believe they go together quite well. When I'm out in the marketplace and I feel the power of the Holy Spirit in my hands, I know the Lord is wanting to do something good. If I make myself available and properly approach the person in need, healing will be released in a very simple way.

There's no striving involved to release power.

Time after time I've noticed how the person in need is also ready to receive healing, so there's no need to convince the person that the Lord can do this for them. The method used to release the gift is not important. I've used a number of different methods in order to confirm how the bible relates different methods of how people were healed.

When I use authority to minister to someone, it often entails laying a proper foundation of truth in order for the person to receive.

Some people who need healing or deliverance need so because they've invited the work of the enemy into their lives through sin or lack of knowledge. When I'm able to properly educate the person on what I believe caused this issue in their life and they understand and receive the counsel, they've just prepared themselves for healing or deliverance through the use of authority. This applies to believers who know better and since it could involve sin, they need to repent of the sin first in order to receive. If they don't need to repent beforehand, it just means there's still ignorance in them in this particular area, so the offense against the Lord isn't as bad as sinning after coming to a knowledge of the truth.

Ignorant people get healed easy because they're ignorant.

They don't truly understand the significance of the sin they're committing. When unbelievers (ignorant people) get healed, it's a sign for them so that they will believe the good news and get saved. The use of authority works well on unbelievers because of their ignorance. I can get the devil off them through authority because the devil has deceived them in their ignorance. It's similar to children getting healed easy because of the ignorance of youth. They haven't had the chance yet to either accept or reject truth.

There are some other points I want to share about the baptism of the Holy Spirit before moving on to the next chapter. Many believers have been taught that the initial evidence of the baptism of the Holy Spirit is speaking in tongues. I understand why this is taught, but I do have a different opinion on this matter.

I've already shared why I believe tongues was the sign on the day of Pentecost. If I'm baptizing someone and they don't break out in tongues after coming up out of the water, does that mean they haven't received the baptism of the Holy Spirit?

Tongues is a sign for unbelievers. If I'm baptizing someone and it's just me and the person I'm baptizing, why would the person break out in a tongue if tongues are meant to get the attention of unbelievers? It makes no sense. I understand if there happens to be an unbeliever there as well who speaks another language. That's usually not the case.

A very clear evidence of the baptism of the Holy Spirit is one that I experienced. Up to the point of being saved, I never read the bible. After receiving the baptism of the Holy Spirit, I gained an insatiable desire to read the bible. The bible itself says that its words are spiritually discerned.

How can I understand the bible without the Spirit if the words are spiritually discerned?

If I'm understanding it, that means I have the Spirit.

NOW WE HAVE RECEIVED, NOT THE SPIRIT OF THE WORLD, BUT THE SPIRIT WHICH IS OF GOD; THAT WE MIGHT KNOW THE THINGS THAT ARE FREELY GIVEN TO US OF GOD.

WHICH THINGS ALSO WE SPEAK, NOT IN THE WORDS WHICH MAN'S WISDOM TEACHETH, BUT WHICH THE HOLY GHOST TEACHETH; COMPARING SPIRITUAL THINGS WITH SPIRITUAL.

BUT THE NATURAL MAN RECEIVETH NOT THE THINGS OF THE SPIRIT OF GOD: FOR THEY ARE FOOLISHNESS UNTO HIM:

NEITHER CAN HE KNOW THEM, BECAUSE THEY ARE SPIRITUALLY DISCERNED.

(1CORINTHIANS 2:12-14)

Earlier I quoted Acts 1:8 in reference to receiving power after that the Holy Spirit comes upon a person. This power enables the believer to walk out this Christian life and the believer becomes a witness for Jesus. Nobody can be a witness for another person's life unless they know the person.

This makes being a witness, evidence of the Holy Spirit.

BUT YE SHALL RECEIVE POWER, AFTER THAT THE HOLY GHOST IS COME UPON YOU: AND YE SHALL BE WITNESSES UNTO ME BOTH IIN JERUSALEM, AND IN ALL JUDAEA, AND IN SAMARIA, AND UNTO THE UTTERMOST PART OF THE EARTH.

(ACTS 1:8)

The baptism of the Holy Spirit is needed for regeneration and to walk out this life as a witness for Jesus.

Gifts are needed to win the lost and encourage believers.

Authority is needed to show the world that Jesus is Lord and that His word is true.

3

THE POWER AND FIRE OF GOD

As I began to minister in healing, I was like a kid in a candy shop for the first time.

I was praying for everyone who would let me. I don't recommend this because people get turned off. I didn't understand why everyone wasn't as excited as I was. This was amazing! How can people not be interested?

If something unique and different happens for you, don't expect everyone to be jumping for joy. Many people were turned off because I was out of control and they had never experienced this before. People are cautious. They get nervous with things that are new and out of the ordinary.

Over the course of time I realized that it's possible to release power without the Lord necessarily being involved in it. He gave me something and I had to learn to steward it.

WISDOM IS THE PRINCIPAL THING;

THEREFORE GET WISDOM:

AND WITH ALL THY GETTING GET UNDERSTANDING.

(PROVERBS 4:7)

The power and fire of God was constantly circulating through me.

When I laid down at night I couldn't sleep. I would lay there buzzing and burning. It felt amazing, but I needed to find the on/off switch.

It may not sound like a good idea to look for and find the off switch, but it had to be done. When you have the scriptures in you with the right perspective, there's no need to worry that the on switch won't be found after you have found the off switch.

FOR THE GIFTS AND CALLING OF GOD ARE WITHOUT REPENTANCE.

(ROMANS 11:29)

God doesn't take back what He gives you.

This doesn't mean the gift can't go dormant. If a believer who is accountable to truth goes back to practicing sin that has been overcome, that believer's faith is being damaged and faith isn't fully released to bring about the desired healing to the person in need. This is because it takes love to truly help someone and faith is released through love. If you're sinning, you're not walking in love.

FOR IN JESUS CHRIST NEITHER CIRCUMCISION AVAILETH ANY THING, NOR UNCIRCUMCISION; BUT FAITH WHICH WORKETH BY LOVE.

(GALATIANS 5:6)

Another reason why the gift can be in you but go dormant, is because the Lord will come to the place of simply not honoring wrong behavior.

Experiencing someone getting healed is an honor, even though it's really the Lord doing the healing through the believer. People that receive healing through my ministry tend to have a certain amount of respect for me because they respect and honor the Lord.

WHEREFORE THE LORD GOD OF ISRAEL SAITH, I SAID INDEED THAT THY HOUSE, AND THE HOUSE OF THY FATHER, SHOULD WALK BEFORE ME FOR EVER:

BUT NOW THE LORD SAITH, BE IT FAR

FROM ME; FOR THEM THAT HONOUR ME I WILL HONOUR, AND THEY THAT DESPISE ME SHALL BE LIGHTLY ESTEEMED.

(1SAMUEL 2:30)

There are ministers who teach that sin in the life of the minister will not prevent the power of God from flowing from that minister to help people. I believe this is wrong.

The reason why many believers cling to this teaching is because the power stops slowly and they don't recognize the lack of results. The Lord doesn't just cut it off. This slow dimming of the power can lead the minister to think that this is just the way it is at this particular time and when people are ready things will start happening again.

I know from my own experience that not fulfilling vows that my own lips spoke will eventually slow the power of God from flowing from me.

You may be wondering how this can be? The Lord puts a huge emphasis on you doing what you said you would do, even if what you promised was rash. This is because God does what He says He will do. The Lord is a promise keeper.

I feel the power of God in my hands and when I repent of not doing what I said I would do, the power I feel in my hands increases.

SUFFER NOT THY MOUTH TO CAUSE THY FLESH TO SIN;

NEITHER SAY THOU BEFORE THE ANGEL, THAT IT WAS AN ERROR:

WHEREFORE SHOULD GOD BE ANGRY AT THY VOICE, AND DESTROY THE WORK OF THINE HANDS?

(ECCLESIASTES 5:6)

At this point in my life (2008), I had already been back in the lawn maintenance business for a number of years. I had no employees. It was just me cutting grass with my lawn mower, trimmer and blower.

Since I worked by myself, I had plenty of time to minister to people during the day. I would pray for customers, people working at pizza shops, gas stations and at many other places that I would frequent.

After awhile I realized that I was getting less and less work done because I was more interested in ministering to people than going to the next job site.

This went on for over a year through the rest of 2008 and all through 2009. I didn't know anyone who ministered like this, although plenty of people at church understood and believed in supernatural healing. At this time I was once again attending Monmouth Worship Center. I was on the altar prayer team and when people would come to the front for prayer I would get the chance to pray for healing. Many people were healed.

I feel the fire of God on my hands everyday. I can be out somewhere and all of a sudden I feel the fire and power course through one, or both of my hands.

When this happens I know Jesus wants to heal someone.

I don't take credit for healing anyone. It's the Lord working through the believer to set captives free.

I simply make myself available for the Lord to use me and when I'm near someone he wishes to minister to, I feel the power.

AND IT CAME TO PASS ON A CERTAIN DAY, AS HE WAS TEACHING, THAT THERE WERE PHARISEES AND DOCTORS OF THE LAW SITTING BY, WHICH WERE COME OUT OF EVERY TOWN OF GALILEE, AND

JUDAEA, AND JERUSALEM:

AND THE POWER OF THE LORD WAS PRESENT TO HEAL THEM.

(LUKE 5:17)

I like to wait on the leading of the Spirit because, I can do nothing on my own.

Just because I can release something doesn't mean the Lord is in it.

THEN ANSWERED JESUS AND SAID UNTO THEM, VERILY, VERILY, I SAY UNTO YOU, THE SON CAN DO NOTHING OF HIMSELF, BUT WHAT HE SEETH THE FATHER DO:

FOR WHAT THINGS SOEVER HE DOETH, THESE ALSO DOETH THE SON LIKEWISE.

(JOHN 5:19)

Earlier when I shared a testimony of the first time I experienced healing I made the point that you don't need to feel any manifest presence of power in your flesh in order to get healed. That's true, but it does seem a bit different when I'm feeling it for someone else.

When I feel the power, I believe it's an angel tapping

my hand to alert me of a ministry situation. This is the Lord saying to me, "Tom, I desire to help this person". Although they don't need to feel anything, something always happens when I feel the power in a certain way. I feel the power in different ways depending on the situation.

A quick tap of power hitting one of my hands is an indication that someone nearby has pain or sickness and it will go away immediately if I minister to the person. This often acts as a type of Geiger Counter. If the person in need is to my left, I will feel the power tap on my left hand and vice versa. If I begin to feel a buildup of power in both hands, it usually means someone is near who needs healing, but it's going take some counseling to help them change some thinking in order to receive.

Just recently, the Lord decided he was going to start challenging me more. When I feel the power of God and/or get a word of knowledge, it's a sure thing something cool is about to happen. The other day I was in a situation where I got several specific words of knowledge and felt the power of God plainly for a woman whom my wife Ahava and I were talking to.

She received and was healed, but it took ministering to her concerning a number of issues in order to get her to receive. I had to hear the Spirit tell me what to address. I'm pretty sure that if I didn't hear clearly, this woman might still be dealing with some pain. Three days later I spoke with her. She's healed and the pain didn't come back.

Sometimes I can tell what the person is feeling by the way the power of God is released. I often say to the person, things like, "You're feeling light, or hot, or tingly, aren't you"?

They're surprised when I know this. I mention these manifestations not because they're needed for the person to be healed, but because they're an attention getter and I want the person to know that I know what's going on in their body.

Many people won't reveal these manifestations even when they're clearly happening to them. Some people think they're strange, so they don't wish to acknowledge what they're feeling, unless I bring it up. The light feeling is because the Lord is taking away a burden. People don't realize how crafty the devil is. He weighs down people slowly so that they don't recognize it happening. When the Lord removes the enemy's burden, the person feels refreshingly light.

The tingly feeling is the result of the power of the Holy Spirit coming upon the flesh. We're all electrical beings and the power of the Holy Spirit is very similar to electricity. Heat represents the cleansing fire of the Lord.

Thousands of people have experienced the fire as I minister to them. Many of them immediately started sweating from the heat. This fire from God has a cleansing nature to it.

WHOSE FAN IS IN HIS HAND, AND HE WILL THROUGHLY PURGE HIS FLOOR, AND GATHER HIS WHEAT INTO THE GARNER; BUT HE WILL BURN UP THE CHAFF WITH UNQUENCHABLE FIRE.

(MATTHEW 3:12)

The chaff is the part of the wheat that is garbage. God burns up the bad stuff in you as you humble yourself before him. He does this because he wants you the way he originally intended you to be.

FOR THE LORD THY GOD IS A CONSUMING FIRE, EVEN A JEALOUS GOD.

(DEUTERONOMY 4:24)

He's jealous because he loves you and wants no part of the devil's work in you, since you are made in his image. He wants back what belongs to him. This fire has some interesting characteristics. I remember going to a hospital to pray for a man struggling with cancer. I stood at the foot of the hospital bed and released this fire towards him. His wife was sitting in a chair about 2 feet to his left.

The fire made a 90 degree turn and hit her and she started to sweat. He felt nothing, but did beat the cancer. I can't explain this, other than that she needed some things burned away. Pain and sickness often leave immediately once the fire of God has gone through the person. These physical manifestations of the Spirit's power on the flesh are often received with reverence. The Lord is looking for reverence and humility.

SURELY HE SCORNETH THE SCORNERS: BUT HE GIVETH GRACE UNTO THE LOWLY.

(PROVERBS 3:34)

James says the same thing using different wording.

BUT HE GIVETH MORE GRACE. WHEREFORE HE SAITH, GOD RESISTETH THE PROUD, BUT GIVETH GRACE UNTO THE HUMBLE.

(JAMES 4: 6)

I remember a certain situation where four men where

being hit by the fire of God and they all got serious and sober minded. One of the guys, in reverence for the presence of the Lord, slowly took his baseball cap off in a reverent way.

4

THE YOUTUBE VIDEOS

In early January of 2010, I went onto YouTube to see if anybody else was doing this healing stuff.

It didn't take long for me to find a guy named Todd White making street healing videos. I thought what Todd was doing was from the people being healed. Immediately, I realized that I wanted to make healing videos because I too, would see many people respond to their healing with a joyful reaction.

HOPE DEFERRED MAKETH THE HEART SICK: BUT WHEN THE DESIRE COMETH, IT IS A TREE OF LIFE.

(PROVERBS 13:12)

I remember it like yesterday when I said to the Lord, "Jesus, I want to make healing videos too, but I don't have the time in my schedule to constantly find someone to hold the camera and record the situation. How can I do this by myself?"

Immediately, the Lord spoke to my spirit and I heard him say, "Go up to people with your camera and get them involved."

I thought that was a brilliant idea. This advice worked immediately when I decided to start making the videos. I bought a Sony Camcorder (which I still have) and when I saw a group of 2, 3, or 4 young people hanging out somewhere, I would approach them with my camera and introduce myself.

Often I would say to them, "Hey guys, can one of you record me on my camera?" As I was saying this, I was holding the camera out for one of them to take. The person would take the camera and usually ask me at the same time, "Sure, what are you doing?" At this point, I would begin to tell them that I pray for people and they get healed. I would say, "Do any of you guys have pain or sickness that won't go away?"

I always spoke with the posture that I was already friends with them and that what I was doing was normal.

One or two would often say, "Yes, I've got pain". Many times I would inadvertently hand the camera off to the guy who needed to be healed. That was a word of knowledge that I wasn't recognizing yet. I would simply take the camera from him and hand it to another guy and say, "Ok, you hold this". He would take the camera, which was already recording and because I gave him a job, he would do it without me directing him.

We live in a sight and sound generation and young people have no problem with cameras. Older folk sometimes freak out when you want to record the situation, so most videos include young people. I prefer ministering to younger people anyway because they're still malleable and I can lay a proper foundation of truth.

Many people like healing videos, but some don't. I don't let the naysayers discourage me from continuing to make them.

LET YOUR LIGHT SO SHINE BEFORE MEN, THAT THEY MAY SEE YOUR GOOD WORKS, AND GLORIFY YOUR FATHER WHICH IS IN HEAVEN.

(MATTHEW 5:16)

I believe the best way to learn something is to see it done by someone else and then go do it yourself. I've made well over 500 videos and they've been viewed millions of times around the world. At one point, the total monthly view count was as high as 60,000 views for all the videos combined.

I've received hundreds of messages over the years from believers who have thanked me for the videos and have testified that they now understand who they are in Christ. They've gained a knowledge of the power of Holy Spirit in them and they tell me how they now get results healing the sick.

THOSE THINGS, WHICH YE HAVE BOTH LEARNED, AND RECEIVED, AND HEARD, AND SEEN IN ME, DO:

AND THE GOD OF PEACE SHALL BE WITH YOU.

(PHILIPPIANS 4:9)

I can't thank the Lord Jesus enough for the privilege and honor of being able to help fellow believers in such an awesome way.

I've come a long way since beginning this video ministry and that can be seen in the videos. As I said earlier, when I first started ministering healing I was out of control because of excitement and ignorance. In my early videos, I spoke very fast and you couldn't shut me up. I still do talk fast, but I've slowed down compared to my early days of ministry. Viewers want to hear what is being said by the person being ministered to and I have to remind myself to talk less so that they can be heard.

There's so much that can be learned from watching a recorded healing situation: Who to minister to.

How to speak. How to listen. What to say. What not to say. When to say it. How long to keep the situation going. How to control the situation so that there are no uncomfortable silences.

What questions to ask.

How to overlook offenses. How to direct the situation. How to follow-up. How to introduce the idea of recording the situation.

When to stop recording.

The list can go on, but I think you get the point. If you watch closely, there's much to learn from watching a healing video.

I believe everyone has a particular circle of influence that makes them effective. After you have spoken with enough people in the marketplace, you will begin to recognize the people that you are influential with.

Surely, we can all minister to any age when we're mature enough in the Lord, but I've found that a certain age group is easier to minister to than other age groups. I like to minister to young men between the ages of 18-23. I do enjoy ministering to women in this age group as well, but only when guy friends are present as well. The legal adult age in America is 18, but I have found that 17 year olds can be just as mature as 18 year olds.

I particularly enjoy it when they display a somewhat joking manner, but they're not out of control with it. This makes it easy for me to get on their level and thereby opening the door for them to receive what I have to offer. If you've done marketplace ministry, you know that people watch you very closely in order to determine if you're the real deal or not.

As I watch my own videos, I can see how the person I'm ministering to is watching me very closely. Usually, I won't look them in the eyes when praying because I know they have a desire to look at my eyes. This makes it more comfortable for them to look at my eyes when I'm not staring back at them.

The YouTube channel is my name, Thomas Fischer. I made a playlist on the channel that highlights videos that I will refer to in this chapter. To find my channel go to YouTube and type Thomas Fischer in the search box. This will bring you to a page with choices that include other channels.

Click on my name and you will be brought to my channel. On the channel homepage there is a link called, Playlists. Click on that link and you will be brought to the Playlists page. Then, click on the link called, Street Healing Book Playlist. As I share with you about certain situations, I will tell you the name of the video that I'm referring to and you will easily find it on the playlist.

Dealing with Ignorance

Some young people have said things that are inappropriate when I ministered to them. This is because of ignorance and you should always overlook ignorance.

Let the person save face if they offend with words. You have to know what battles to engage in. If a young person starts cursing, I overlook this because if I corrected this wrong behavior at that moment, it could put a wall up between us and prevent the healing from being received. To make this point clear, there's a video which shows the positive effects of overlooking offenses. Actually, the whole effect of this is seen in two different videos.

I uploaded a video where a young man begins to unleash a barrage of F-bombs in response to being healed of Scoliosis. All his friends laughed and so did I. I don't condone cursing, but it wasn't the time to correct this ignorance.

The video is called, "Scoliosis Healed" and it's included in the playlist. Months later, I came across this young man and he was very happy to see me and tell me that he no longer has Scoliosis and that his doctor said he doesn't need the scheduled surgery to try and fix it.

AND ABOVE ALL THINGS HAVE FERVENT CHARITY AMONG YOURSELVES:

FOR CHARITY SHALL COVER THE MULTITUDE OF SINS.

(1PETER 4:8)

There's another situation on video where a young man is offensive with cursing and blasphemy, but he was doing it in a non-aggressive way. I let him save face. In this particular video, his friend was healed of pain in his hand. The young man engaging me with curse words was trying to ignore his friend who was saying that the pain had gone away after I ministered. I didn't insist that he stop his barrage of foul words in order to hear his friend's testimony. This is because I felt as if he knew the healing had happened but was ignoring his friend for fear of being embarrassed because what I said would happen, did happen.

I overlooked the offense. Treating him this way would free him to consider Jesus in the future. This video is called, "Dirty Mouth Of Unbelief" and it's included in the playlist.

As I made healing videos, I started to realize that videos are a good way to confirm God's word. Jesus said He confirms His word with signs.

AND THEY WENT FORTH, AND PREACHED EVERY WHERE, THE LORD WORKING WITH THEM,

AND CONFIRMING THE WORD WITH SIGNS FOLLOWING. AMEN.

(MARK 16:20)

<u>Healing with Objects</u>

Being a student of the bible, I noticed how the power of God was transferred into objects and those objects now held the power to heal.

The bible calls these special miracles.

AND GOD WROUGHT SPECIAL MIRACLES

BY THE HANDS OF PAUL:

SO THAT FROM HIS BODY WERE BROUGHT UNTO THE SICK HANDKERCHIEFS OR APRONS,

AND THE DISEASES DEPARTED FROM THEM, AND THE EVIL SPIRITS WENT OUT OF THEM.

(ACTS 19:11-12)

I decided that the Lord would do the same thing through me. One day when I was at a local convenience store I saw a group of young people entering the store. I decided to hang out in the parking lot and wait for them to come out so that I could try out this miracle.

I picked up a stick and quickly prayed over it, asking the Holy Spirit to fill it with His power so that whoever took it in hand would then be healed. The rest is history. You can see the situation on video. The video is called, "Healed By A Stick" and it's included in the playlist.

Shadow Healing

In Acts 5:15 we see Peter's shadow healing people.

INSOMUCH THAT THEY BROUGHT FORTH THE SICK INTO THE STREETS, AND LAID THEM ON BEDS AND COUCHES,

THAT AT THE LEAST THE SHADOW OF PETER PASSING BY MIGHT OVERSHADOW SOME OF THEM.

(ACTS 5:15)

I know from scripture that I have the same Spirit in me that Peter had in him, so I could experience this miracle as well.

BUT IF THE SPIRIT OF HIM THAT RAISED UP JESUS FROM THE DEAD DWELL IN YOU,

HE THAT RAISED UP CHRIST FROM THE DEAD SHALL ALSO QUICKEN YOUR MORTAL BODIES BY HIS SPIRIT THAT DWELLETH IN YOU.

(ROMANS 8:11)

As I was out and about looking for my next healing situation, I decided I would take a leap of faith and use my shadow to heal.

Since that first time, I've used my shadow many times to minister healing. The video is called, "First Shadow

Healing" and it's included in the playlist.

Confirming God's Word

There are many ways to confirm the authenticity of God's word. For instance, we have been given authority over the enemy and so one day I thought I would make it abundantly clear just how true this is. Most people can attest to how it's possible to know what someone is saying just by looking at the person's face. This applies mostly to a mother or father's look of authority.

I believe demons understand this authority, so I decided I would look at pain with a look of authority and it would go away. I've done this healing miracle a number of times. I recorded the first such instance. The video is on the playlist and it's called, "Casting Out Demons With A Look Of Authority".

WHEN HE SAW JESUS, HE CRIED OUT, AND FELL DOWN BEFORE HIM, AND WITH A LOUD VOICE SAID,

WHAT HAVE I TO DO WITH THEE, JESUS, THOU SON OF GOD MOST HIGH? I BESEECH THEE, TORMENT ME NOT.

(LUKE 8:28)

Unexpected Blessings

Over the years I've met many great brothers and sisters in the Lord because of the YouTube videos I've made. The first person I ever met who also ministered healing was Joel Jackson. We quickly became friends.

On one particular video, which I have since deleted (I can't remember why), I held my ministry card up to the camera and Joel paused the video and read the phone number on the card. He called me and we got to talking and have had dozens of conversations since then and have ministered together a couple times as well. Joel and I learned a lot about healing from each other as we would bounce ideas and testimonies off each other.

The first overseas ministry trip I went on was to England. The trip was sponsored by Robert Taylor. Robert saw the videos I was producing and he invited me, along with Pete Cabrera Jr. to come minister on the streets together with a number of other believers. Pete is an amazing minister with a strong belief of his identity in Christ. He sets captives free everywhere he goes and trains believers all over the world to do the same.

Robert is a very unique man of God with a gentle, compassionate approach to helping people. We quickly became good friends and still are today. In fact, he asked me to be the Best Man at his wedding and I was honored to accept.

John Latini is another amazing man of God who has seen the Lord do countless miracles in the marketplace as well as in the church that he pastors. One day a number of years ago, after he saw my videos he contacted me for healing prayer as well as prayer for getting started in ministry because he felt a strong calling on his life to minister in the supernatural. He got healed and quickly began seeing miracles. He's been a source of great encouragement to many. When he and his wife Sue Ellen renewed their wedding vows, John asked me if I would be the minister who performed the ceremony for them. I was honored to accept the invitation.

Tim Curwen, who wrote the Foreword to this book, saw one of my videos. After watching it, he gave his life to the Lord as a result of seeing the Lord's power and love on display in the video. The video that led to this conversion is the most popular one I've made and is called, "MUST WATCH DRAMATIC NEW YORK HEALING AND SALVATION" and it's included in the playlist. Tim and his wife Maria and their children have become very good friends with Ahava and I. They invited us over to Scotland, where they live and we enjoyed fellowship with them and their children as we shared with them what we've learned from the Lord up to that point.

One day over 5 years ago, a brother in the Lord from Canada contacted me because he had been watching my videos. Doug Collins and his wife Donna have been a tremendous blessing to us ever since. Doug gets great results ministering healing as well as training believers on the streets of Windsor, Ontario. He's also a brilliant business man and has helped me a lot in many ways, along with ordering my ministry in a way that enables me to continue doing this full time.

Only a few hours before writing this, I sent a text to Rock Mcilvain. He and his wife Angela have been a great blessing to us. I sensed I needed to contact him and after I did, he wrote back that he had been thinking of me yesterday and today.

That's the spiritual connection that is made with brothers and sisters in the Lord when friendship is developed. Rock first saw my videos many years ago and contacted me because he knew of nobody else who did healing miracles. He has experienced the Lord doing lots of miracles and wanted to talk with someone like-minded. Since then, we have seen them a number of times.

A number of years ago when I was ministering in

Tucson, AZ, a brother named Tom Hackley saw my videos and was surprised to see that I was currently in Tucson. He and his wife Janet live relatively close to Tucson, so he asked to meet up. I said sure and we met. This was before I was married, so Ahava wasn't with me. They brought me lunch and we had a good time of fellowship and ministering to some people in Tucson. They have been a tremendous blessing to both Ahava and I for years.

I can go on and on listing the names of believers who I've met over the years because of the videos. Andy from the channel, Firecharger. Brian from the channel, OT4Jesus. David Higgins. Dustin from the channel, streetministries seven.

Speaking of Tucson, I'm reminded of an adventure the Lord sent me on that led me out west from New Jersey. It was the fall of 2012 and I received a phone call from a brother in the Lord who'd been watching the videos. Bobby Toman lives on Long Island in New York and he messaged me and asked me if I wanted an old RV (recreational vehicle) he had. I quickly said yes because for years I had a dream of traveling across America in an RV as an evangelist. It's amazing how the Lord will bring to pass the desires of your heart even if you're not thinking about them. I traveled to Bobby's home 3 weekends in a row to do some minor repairs with him to the RV. On the third weekend I was ready to drive it home.

About a month later and the day Hurricane Sandy ended, I embarked on my journey south. What an adventure! I ministered all along the way as I traveled south from New Jersey to Atlanta and then west to Arizona where I enjoyed the warm winter weather. I made a number of healing videos along the way and particularly in Arizona. One of the videos is called, "Symptoms of Mono leave and they believe on Jesus". The video is on the, Street Healing Book Playlist.

The greatest blessing I've received from the Lord besides salvation occurred in December of 2012 when I was in Tucson, AZ. I noticed on Facebook that a beautiful young lady named Mahira had posted one of my videos on her Facebook page. I thought it was a good idea to strike up a conversation with her because she was a Christian besides being beautiful. She agreed to talk to me on FaceTime.

On that very first call, I told her that she should come to America and marry me. She thought to herself that it was very rude and inappropriate, but didn't express it at the time. After we ended our talk and I laid down for the night I asked the Lord to show me something about Mahira that nobody else knew because that would show her that I was a legitimate man of God. I promptly had a vision and heard the Lord speak to me about Mahira.

The next day we talked on Skype and I shared my experience with her. She was shocked when I shared the vision and what the Lord said concerning her.

Later, she said the blood drained from her face and she felt weak because it was true and only 2 people in the world knew this information. That helped me repair the thought she had of thinking I was rude to ask her to marry me the first day I spoke with her.

Since then she has legally changed her name to Ahava Sarah because she is a new creation in the Lord.

WHOSO FINDETH A WIFE FINDETH A GOOD THING, AND OBTAINETH FAVOUR OF THE LORD.

(PROVERBS 18:22)

5
UNIQUE MANIFESTATIONS

Cold Hand Hot Hand

I share about unique manifestations because they can happen for you by hearing the testimonies and believing for them to occur in your ministry.

The Holy Spirit is very unique with the manifestations of his power. Early in my ministry the Lord started doing something that I thought was odd. This particular manifestation made a very clear point about forgiveness.

I call it the hot hand, cold hand thing. Many times while laying my hand on a person's shoulder to pray, they would feel heat. Sometimes the person would feel a cold sensation.

The Spirit revealed to me the meaning of this manifestation. The Spirit doesn't withhold the wisdom that comes from the Father because we need it in order to bring healing to people.

The hot feeling is good and means the person is receiving. The cold feeling means the person needs to forgive. The scripture is clear that we must forgive those who have offended us.

AND BECAUSE INIQUITY SHALL ABOUND,

THE LOVE OF MANY SHALL WAX COLD.

(MATTHEW 24:12)

When I'm ministering and feeling a cold sensation while placing my hand on the person's shoulder, I will begin to interview the person and ask who they need to forgive. With my hand still on them and confession of the sin being made, my hand will go from cold to hot and the pain will go away, usually without addressing the pain.

I've made a healing video that shows this manifestation occurring and the resulting healing that comes from forgiveness. The video is called, Cold Hand Hot Hand and it is on the playlist.

The cold thing can be tricky sometimes because there is another reason why people feel cold. The manifestation of cold isn't just because someone has become spiritually cold and needs to forgive.

Supernatural Icepack

Sometimes the manifestation is what I call, a supernatural icepack. Once this manifestation started to happen the Spirit gave me revelation. Since ice in the natural makes swelling and inflammation go away, the Spirit will manifest a cold sensation for swelling and inflammation to go away supernaturally.

I was at a house meeting and a pastor asked me to pray for him because he had non-stop pain in his neck at the base of the brain stem. He was in a car accident many years earlier. Many people had prayed for him over the years to no avail. I laid my hand on his neck and immediately began to feel a lot of cold, even before I began to say anything. At first I thought he needed to forgive someone, but that wasn't the case.

Then I realized he was getting a supernatural icepack, so I agreed with this by proclaiming it. He got healed. I emailed him a week later and he was still healed. The pain never came back. He dealt with that injury non-stop for years.

Having the right perspective of the word of God will bring the manifestation of the Spirit's power in a way that some believers don't realize. Inaccurate teaching in the body of Christ stifles the flow of the Spirit's power.

MAKING THE WORD OF GOD OF NONE EFFECT THROUGH YOUR TRADITION,

WHICH YE HAVE DELIVERED: AND MANY SUCH LIKE THINGS DO YE.

(MARK 7:13)

One example of wrong teaching is when Christians ask God to send his glory. I understand and agree there are moves of the Spirit that radically change lives for the good, but many believers seem to be waiting on these moves as if they aren't equip to do the work of ministry until they have these experiences.

I was in a healing situation with two Christian women that needed prayer to be free of worry.

I told them the glory of the Lord fills the whole earth.

FOR THE EARTH SHALL BE FILLED WITH THE KNOWLEDGE OF THE GLORY OF THE LORD, AS THE WATERS COVER THE SEA.

(HABAKKUK 2:14)

After explaining this to them, I had both of them take two deep breaths. The glory of the Lord filled them and a calming peace came on them. I also took two deep breaths and so did Michael Brown, who was recording the situation with my iPhone. Both Michael and I felt the power of the Lord and it caused us both to feel calm and relaxed even though neither of us were stressed out.

Interestingly, neither of the women took very deep breaths as you might picture a deep breath, but yet, they received. You can watch the video called, "Breath Deep The Gathering Glory" on the playlist. Unlike the lyrics, "Breathe deep the gathering gloom", by the Moody Blues, I prefer a more positive outlook.

When I first started feeling the power of the Holy Spirit in my hands, it was very unique in that it felt like nails about to pierce through the palms of my hands.

BEHOLD, I HAVE GRAVEN THEE UPON THE PALMS OF MY HANDS...

(ISAIAH 49:16)

Stigmata

I learned from study that this is called "Stigmata". Many believers don't agree with this, but it happened to me many times. It actually hurt, but in a way that I welcomed, if that makes sense. I never fully received stigmata, although I considered it an honor and welcomed it, because the word of God testifies to who we are in Christ when we believe what he has done for us.

I AM CRUCIFIED WITH CHRIST:

NEVERTHELESS I LIVE; YET NOT I, BUT CHRIST LIVETH IN ME:

AND THE LIFE WHICH I NOW LIVE IN THE FLESH I LIVE BY THE FAITH OF THE SON OF GOD, WHO LOVED ME, AND GAVE HIMSELF FOR ME.

(GALATIANS 2:20)

Although I wanted this unique manifestation, I believe it never fully manifested because I was double- minded.

I love working out with weights and would wonder how I would be able to workout with painful wounds in the palms of my hands. Perhaps another reason why this never fully manifested was because I've always been someone who worked hard with my hands in the workplace and in serving.

A log in Heaven

Probably the most amazing manifestation that has occurred for me involved a 5 year old girl who died and went to heaven.

I was in Texas ministering when I got a phone call from a friend I hadn't spoken to in years. Her daughter was in a Philadelphia hospital and she wanted me to come there to pray for her. I couldn't go at that moment because I was on a ministry trip that was paid for by the people who invited me to Texas.

I told my friend that I would pray for her daughter that night and then come to Philadelphia in a few days when I returned. That night something strange happened.

When I awoke, I had a burning pain on my chest and knew the child had died.

I went into the hotel bathroom and was astonished to see a footprint on my chest. I took a picture of the footprint. I received a vision from the Lord of what happened to cause this footprint, which I knew belonged to the child.

The Lord brought me to heaven and laid me down in a grassy field as a log. This child, who was constantly tormented by demons, died and was fleeing the grasp of these demons.

She jumped onto me, being a log and into the arms of Jesus.

About a week later I was in the home of the parents

talking to the dad. He was barefooted and I noticed that he had toes with spaces in between them that was more than the usual amount of space between toes.

The footprint on my chest was the same unique type of foot. I said to the dad, "Your daughter has the same foot as you."

He replied, "Yes, she does."

He showed me one of her shoes and it was the same size as the footprint on my chest.

6
THE ROLE OF FORGIVENESS

There's a misconception that has developed through the healing videos. I've made well over 500 videos and most of them showcase someone getting healed immediately without regard to any wrong behavior or thinking they may be engaging in.

There's a reason why the people in my videos receive healing quick and easy. Healing is an evangelistic tool. Jesus didn't heal people just because it's in his nature to heal. He also healed people so that they would believe in him.

IF I DO NOT THE WORKS OF MY FATHER, BELIEVE ME NOT.

BUT IF I DO, THOUGH YE BELIEVE NOT ME, BELIEVE THE WORKS:

THAT YE MAY KNOW, AND BELIEVE, THAT

THE FATHER IS IN ME, AND I IN HIM.

(JOHN 10:37-38)

When healing is being used as an evangelistic tool, it's easy to get people healed because of the ignorance in them. This is not the case with believers who know better. There's an accountability that comes with knowledge.

NEVERTHELESS, WHERETO WE HAVE ALREADY ATTAINED,

LET US WALK BY THE SAME RULE,

LET US MIND THE SAME THING.

(PHILIPPIANS 3:16)

Philippians 3:16 means, let us live up to what we've already attained. The verse is showing us there's accountability to what we know. When a person turns from going their own way in life and turns to the Lord, the process of sanctification begins. Every new believer is disciplined by the Lord.

FOR WHOM THE LORD LOVETH HE CHASTENETH, AND SCOURGETH EVERY SON WHOM HE RECEIVETH.

(HEBREWS 12:6)

Jesus does this so that people won't perish. When believers who have truth in them, harden their hearts towards the Lord's word and refuse to forgive, they have made themselves susceptible to destruction.

This is clearly seen in scripture. I believe the best case for this is found in the story of the unmerciful servant.

THEN CAME PETER TO HIM, AND SAID, LORD, HOW OFT SHALL MY BROTHER SIN AGAINST ME, AND I FORGIVE HIM? TILL SEVEN TIMES?

JESUS SAITH UNTO HIM, I SAY NOT UNTO THEE, UNTIL SEVEN TIMES: BUT, UNTIL SEVENTY TIMES SEVEN.

THEREFORE IS THE KINGDOM OF HEAVEN LIKENED UNTO A CERTAIN KING, WHICH WOULD TAKE ACCOUNT OF HIS SERVANTS. AND WHEN HE HAD BEGUN TO RECKON, ONE WAS BROUGHT UNTO HIM, WHICH OWED HIM TEN THOUSAND TALENTS.

BUT FORASMUCH AS HE HAD NOT TO PAY, HIS LORD COMMANDED HIM TO BE SOLD, AND HIS WIFE, AND CHILDREN, AND ALL THAT HE HAD, AND PAYMENT TO BE

MADE.

THE SERVANT THEREFORE FELL DOWN, AND WORSHIPPED HIM, SAYING, LORD, HAVE PATIENCE WITH ME, AND I WILL PAY THEE ALL.

THEN THE LORD OF THAT SERVANT WAS MOVED WITH COMPASSION, AND LOOSED HIM, AND FORGAVE HIM THE DEBT. BUT THE SAME SERVANT WENT OUT, AND FOUND ONE OF HIS FELLOWSERVANTS, WHICH OWED HIM AN HUNDRED PENCE: AND HE LAID HANDS ON HIM, AND TOOK HIM BY THE THROAT, SAYING, PAY ME THAT THOU OWEST.

AND HIS FELLOWSERVANT FELL DOWN AT HIS FEET, AND BESOUGHT HIM, SAYING, HAVE PATIENCE WITH ME, AND I WILL PAY THEE ALL. AND HE WOULD NOT: BUT WENT AND CAST HIM INTO PRISON, TILL HE SHOULD PAY THE DEBT.

SO WHEN HIS FELLOWSERVANTS SAW WHAT WAS DONE, THEY WERE VERY SORRY, AND CAME AND TOLD UNTO THEIR LORD ALL THAT WAS DONE.

THEN HIS LORD, AFTER THAT HE HAD CALLED HIM, SAID UNTO HIM, O THOU WICKED SERVANT, I FORGAVE THEE ALL THAT DEBT, BECAUSE THOU DESIREDST ME:

SHOULDEST NOT THOU ALSO HAVE HAD COMPASSION ON THY FELLOWSERVANT, EVEN AS I HAD PITY ON THEE?

AND HIS LORD WAS WROTH, AND DELIVERED HIM TO THE TORMENTORS, TILL HE SHOULD PAY ALL THAT WAS DUE UNTO HIM.

SO LIKEWISE SHALL MY HEAVENLY FATHER DO ALSO UNTO YOU, IF YE FROM YOUR HEARTS FORGIVE NOT EVERY ONE HIS BROTHER THEIR TRESPASSES.

(MATTHEW 18:21-35)

In this account, Jesus teaches us how to be able to enter the Kingdom of Heaven. Jesus is saying that if you want to go to Heaven make sure you don't behave as the unmerciful servant did. The grace that was extended to him was taken back.

This flies in the face of the, once saved always saved, doctrine.

I say all this to make the point that we must extend forgiveness if we wish to receive forgiveness from the Lord.

When someone claims to believe the gospel message, they're agreeing to always forgive. If someone who claims to be a believer refuses to forgive, they're not a believer because they're not believing the true message of the gospel. I know that's strong language on my part, but the scripture says this.

THEY PROFESS THAT THEY KNOW GOD;

BUT IN WORKS THEY DENY HIM, BEING ABOMINABLE, AND DISOBEDIENT, AND UNTO EVERY GOOD WORK REPROBATE.

(TITUS 1:16)

When a person won't forgive, that person is denying the message.

This is why it's impossible to get a believer healed who has turned from the truth by not forgiving someone. When they repent, the healing comes. I've heard well known ministers say healing can't be stopped because someone is not forgiving. That's wrong teaching.

Ministers who teach this are either afraid to confront people with the truth or they themselves don't recognize this truth. I've been in plenty of ministry situations in the marketplace that plainly show this truth.

I will share with you a couple of good examples, but before I do, I want to make a statement about how I receive my doctrinal understanding. I don't get into ministry situations and then develop an understanding of scripture to back up my experience. That would be wrong.

What I do is, I develop a clear understanding of scripture with proper exegesis using the preponderance of scripture and then I take note of how this understanding is brought to light in my ministry experiences.

STUDY TO SHEW THYSELF APPROVED UNTO GOD,

A WORKMAN THAT NEEDETH NOT TO BE ASHAMED,

RIGHTLY DIVIDING THE WORD OF TRUTH.

(2TIMOTHY 2:15)

One day I went into a pizza restaurant for lunch.

The guys working behind the counter all know me and have been healed of various ailments in the past. I'm standing at the counter and I feel the power of the Holy Spirit. I ask the guys if any of them have pain or sickness. They all smile and say no. I thought that was odd since I felt the power of God.

Then I notice a woman standing to my left that I didn't see at first. "Oh, I didn't see you standing there! Do you need healing?" I asked. She said no, but I could see that she lacked peace, so I asked if she wanted me to pray for peace. In a not-so-excited way, she said yes. I prayed for the peace of the Lord to come upon her and when I got done, I was blasted by an enormous amount of peace.

I almost fell down. "Wow, I feel drunk right now," I exclaimed!

I turned to the guys behind the counter and they were all laughing. I turned to the woman and she looked like she'd been sucking on lemons.

Immediately, the Spirit brought scripture to my remembrance.

AND INTO WHATSOEVER HOUSE YE ENTER,

FIRST SAY, PEACE BE TO THIS HOUSE.

AND IF THE SON OF PEACE BE THERE, YOUR PEACE SHALL REST UPON IT:

IF NOT, IT SHALL TURN TO YOU AGAIN.

(LUKE 10:5-6)

As it turns out, she was a professing Christian, but was mad at her husband and didn't want to forgive him. The point is very clear.

THERE IS NO PEACE, SAITH THE LORD, UNTO THE WICKED.

(ISAIAH 48:22)

I'm not being quick to condemn this woman. She needed to forgive her husband. If she doesn't want to be labeled as wicked, she needs to turn away from hypocrisy and forgive.

On the other hand, I was excited to know that I was releasing a lot of peace. Peace is the main manifestation people feel when I pray for them.

The reason why ignorant unbelievers get healed easily is because of their ignorance of the truth. The Lord is not holding them accountable for their sin at that time.

IF I HAD NOT COME AND SPOKEN UNTO THEM, THEY HAD NOT HAD SIN:

BUT NOW THEY HAVE NO CLOAK FOR THEIR SIN.

(JOHN 15:22)

When I approach an unbeliever, I usually start by asking if they have any pain or sickness that won't go away. I don't go up to people and start preaching the bible to them. That approach doesn't work well because they usually aren't aware of their need. However, if there's something wrong with them, they're aware of that and when they get healed, they're all ears.

AND THE PEOPLE WITH ONE ACCORD GAVE HEED UNTO THOSE THINGS WHICH PHILIP SPAKE,

HEARING AND SEEING THE MIRACLES WHICH HE DID.

(ACTS 8:6)

After I've gotten their attention with the power of God, they're now open to hearing the good news. However, sometimes young unbelievers are aware of the need to forgive, which makes me wonder if they really are unbelievers. I had an interesting experience in Germany once that makes the point clear about the power of forgiving.

I was ministering in the market area of Frankfurt, Germany with Tom and Miriam Penzel. After a couple hours of ministering, we sat down in the the middle of the town square to take a rest. However, I couldn't resist the urge to go talk to a young man sitting about 20 feet away. I told Tom and Miriam I was going go talk to him and they said, "Ok, let us know if you want us to join you after you've shared with him what you want to share."

I approached this young man and introduced myself and what I do. He introduces himself as Sebastian. He's 20 years old, an atheist and doesn't believe in supernatural healing. I responded by asking him if he'd ever felt peace in a physical way and he said no. I asked him if he would like to feel this peace. Everyone, including atheists wants peace. He said yes, so I put my hand out in front of him and called for the peace of Jesus to come upon him.

He felt nothing, which is odd because he's a young, ignorant unbeliever. As I've said many times when teaching people, ignorant unbelievers get healed easily because they're not accountable yet for the sin in their lives. However, as it turns out, he had some truth in him.

Immediately, I got a word of knowledge that he was mad at someone and he admitted that he was mad at his dad. I asked him why he was mad at his dad. He said his dad left home 10 years earlier without any warning and he hadn't seen or heard from him since.

"Wow!" I exclaimed. I told him I understood why he would be mad at his dad for doing such a thing, but I also sensed that he understood the need to forgive and if he ever wanted to see his dad again, the best thing to do would be to forgive him and pray for him.

He confessed that he did believe it was important to forgive. Remember, this young man claimed to be an atheist. Most young atheist are not really atheist, but rather, people with a lack of knowledge.

We both asked God to forgive his dad for doing this. I led him to confess a few things and to verbally express that he forgives his dad. We also asked the Lord to bless his dad.

After this I told Sebastian that I would pray again for him to experience the peace of God in a physical way.

I prayed the same way I did at first, but only this time the power of God slammed this kid. He started sweating and getting goose bumps up and down his arms.

With great enthusiasm he says, "Wow, that's real!"

I asked him if he believed now and he said yes. I explained the gospel to him and led him in a prayer to receive Christ. He was so happy.

At this point I call over Tom and Miriam Penzel and they start to share with him what's on their heart. Tom Penzel prayed for Sebastian to receive the baptism of the Holy Spirit and immediately afterwards beautiful church bells start ringing in the town square.

The timing was perfect.

I looked at Sebastian and said to him, "Sebastian, that's for you. The bible says that when someone turns to the Lord, the angels in heaven rejoice." A big smile came on his face.

LIKEWISE, I SAY UNTO YOU,

THERE IS JOY IN THE PRESENCE OF THE ANGELS OF GOD OVER ONE SINNER THAT REPENTETH.

(LUKE 15:10)

7
WHEN PAIN COMES BACK

Sometimes after a person gets healed, the pain comes back. I believe there are several reasons for this. The most common reason, I believe, is doubt in the person needing to be healed.

BUT LET HIM ASK IN FAITH, NOTHING WAVERING. FOR HE THAT WAVERETH IS LIKE A WAVE OF THE SEA DRIVEN WITH THE WIND AND TOSSED. FOR LET NOT THAT MAN THINK THAT HE SHALL RECEIVE ANY THING OF THE LORD.

(JAMES 1:6-7)

Often, people in need don't think they're doubting, but they don't recognize tiny seeds of doubt in them. People struggle with doubt for a number of reasons. The main reason, I believe, is due to poor decisions in the past. Poor decision making leads to poor results.

Poor results in any goal or task leads to doubt. As the scripture states, this person shouldn't expect to receive anything from the Lord.

However, I have noticed, if pain goes away once, it will go away many times, until the person in need believes enough to hold onto the healing. Each time the person receives the power of the Lord and the pain leaves, the doubt is diminishing because the results remain consistent. Consistent results kill doubt. The person eventually gets to the point where they believe the healing is for them.

I've noticed that some people who have to receive many times before the pain stays gone are people who have a guilty conscience from past sins. Once they have truly repented and realize their sins are forgiven, the guilt begins to leave. Not believing you're truly forgiven can also stem from legalistic teaching that puts condemnation on people each time they make a mistake.

Sometimes pain comes back because of concealed sin or pride in a person's life. This applies to the believer who knows better and is therefore accountable. It doesn't apply to the ignorant unbeliever, although pain can come back on the ignorant unbeliever because of the previous example of doubt.

JESUS SAID UNTO THEM, IF YE WERE BLIND, YE SHOULD HAVE NO SIN: BUT NOW YE SAY, WE SEE; THEREFORE YOUR SIN REMAINETH.

(JOHN 9:41)

Another scripture that shows this truth is in Proverbs.

HE THAT COVERETH HIS SINS SHALL NOT PROSPER: BUT WHOSO CONFESSETH AND FORSAKETH THEM SHALL HAVE MERCY.

(PROVERBS 28:13)

Some Christians teach that mercy is not getting what you deserve. That's true to an extent, but they tend to leave out the repentance part. This proverb shows that mercy comes when you repent and renounce sins. In other words, you don't get mercy just because you ask for it. You get mercy when you repent. You also get mercy when you are always merciful.

BLESSED ARE THE MERCIFUL: FOR THEY SHALL OBTAIN MERCY.

(MATTHEW 5:7)

Some people have a hard time believing the Lord has forgiven them after they've repented. The bible makes no distinction between healing and the forgiveness of sins. If Jesus has forgiven you, healing belongs to you. The scripture lumps healing and forgiveness together.

BLESS THE LORD, O MY SOUL: AND ALL THAT IS WITHIN ME, BLESS HIS HOLY NAME. BLESS THE LORD, O MY SOUL, AND FORGET NOT ALL HIS BENEFITS: WHO FORGIVETH ALL THINE INIQUITIES; WHO HEALETH ALL THY DISEASES;

(PSALM 103:1-3)

The opposite also applies. If Jesus hasn't forgiven your sins, your not healed. The Greek word Sozo means, to save from death, disease, destruction, etc. The forgiveness of sins is linked to healing. If a person is not forgiven, they're not healed. Unbelievers get healed before getting saved because the Lord is trying to get them to believe that He has forgiven them.

Some Christians believe Jesus has already forgiven the sins of the whole world, so that means healing is for them. This is true positionally, not experientially.

Jesus has atoned for the sins of the whole world, but forgiveness of sins is appropriated through repentance and that's why repentance is needed for healing to come to the person who has become accountable.

For the ignorant person, healing will come first and this often leads to repentance.

OR DESPISEST THOU THE RICHES OF HIS GOODNESS AND FORBEARANCE AND LONGSUFFERING;

NOT KNOWING THAT THE GOODNESS OF GOD LEADETH THEE TO REPENTANCE?

(ROMANS 2:4)

When believers get healed before repenting of some sin, it simply means there's still ignorance that the Lord recognizes in that particular area of the believer's life in Christ.

Sometimes pain comes back because the minister is releasing power, but the Lord is not doing the work yet. In other words, the minister is running ahead of the Lord. It's easy to miss the Lord if your always in a hurry. The Lord has had to tell me a number of times to slow down. Timing is a biblical principle.

FOR THIS IS THE WORD OF PROMISE, AT THIS TIME WILL I COME, AND SARAH SHALL HAVE A SON.

(ROMANS 9:9)

Some Christians think the whole timing thing is old covenant thinking. If that's true, why didn't Jesus heal the crippled man at the gate beautiful? Surely the man was lying there when Jesus went through the gate. God's timing doesn't mean He's withholding something good from you.

The right perspective is what's needed when considering any of God's ways that seem confusing. Often, the person in need of healing needs to change some thinking in order to receive. This is why the healing of the soul is most important. When the soul is healed, the body often lines up with that right mindset.

BELOVED, I WISH ABOVE ALL THINGS THAT THOU MAYEST PROSPER AND BE IN HEALTH,

EVEN AS THY SOUL PROSPERETH.

(3JOHN 1:2)

If it takes time for the soul (mind, will and emotions) to heal, there's definitely a timing issue.

TO EVERY THING THERE IS A SEASON,

AND A TIME TO EVERY PURPOSE UNDER THE HEAVEN:

A TIME TO BE BORN, AND A TIME TO DIE;

A TIME TO PLANT, AND A TIME TO PLUCK UP THAT WHICH IS PLANTED;

A TIME TO KILL, AND A TIME TO HEAL;

A TIME TO BREAK DOWN, AND A TIME TO BUILD UP;

A TIME TO WEEP, AND A TIME TO LAUGH;

A TIME TO MOURN, AND A TIME TO DANCE;

A TIME TO CAST AWAY STONES, AND A TIME TO GATHER STONES TOGETHER;

A TIME TO EMBRACE, AND A TIME TO REFRAIN FROM EMBRACING;

A TIME TO GET, AND A TIME TO LOSE;

A TIME TO KEEP, AND A TIME TO CAST AWAY; A

TIME TO REND, AND A TIME TO SEW;

A TIME TO KEEP SILENCE, AND A TIME TO SPEAK;

A TIME TO LOVE, AND A TIME TO HATE;

A TIME OF WAR, AND A TIME OF PEACE.

(ECCLESIASTES 3:1-8)

I'm not trying to make excuses for not getting someone healed. I admit to not getting everyone healed. In some healing situations I failed to release the faith needed for a person that was ready to receive.

If the Lord is telling me to say this or that in order for the person to receive and I am failing to hear Him because of my own spiritual dullness, then I'm the one failing; even though the timing is right for this person to be healed.

Sometimes pain comes back because there are other spiritual doors that need to be closed. For example, I was in a healing situation where pain came back and then I got a word of knowledge that the person needed to make up with her mom. She repented and asked the Lord for forgiveness and for her mom to be blessed.

After this, I ministered and again the pain left. Then the pain came back again. I got another word of knowledge that she needed to repent of fornicating. She repented and I ministered to her and again the pain left.

Only this time it didn't come back. She was healed.

Some Christians don't think there's scriptural basis for pain or sickness coming back because there are no examples in the bible of pain or sickness coming back. However, we do see Jesus teaching about demons coming back after being cast out.

WHEN THE UNCLEAN SPIRIT IS GONE OUT OF A MAN, HE WALKETH THROUGH DRY PLACES,

SEEKING REST, AND FINDETH NONE.

THEN HE SAITH, I WILL RETURN INTO MY HOUSE FROM WHENCE I CAME OUT;

AND WHEN HE IS COME, HE FINDETH IT EMPTY, SWEPT, AND GARNISHED.

THEN GOETH HE, AND TAKETH WITH HIMSELF SEVEN OTHER SPIRITS MORE WICKED THAN HIMSELF, AND THEY ENTER IN AND DWELL THERE:

AND THE LAST STATE OF THAT MAN IS WORSE THAN THE FIRST.

EVEN SO SHALL IT BE ALSO UNTO THIS WICKED GENERATION.

(MATTHEW 12:43-45)

In this portion of scripture the point that's being made is that the person who gets delivered from a demon needs to get the word of God in them, so that when the demons come back, they're turned off because they can tell the person has gotten the word in them.

Demons want no part of anyone who has the word of God in them. You can take my bible away, but it's too late because I already got it in me. I've been reading it consistently for over 25 years and often go to sleep with audio bible playing.

Many healing situations in the bible were people that needed deliverance from a demon, in order to be healed of pain or sickness. In the next chapter I will share a story of deliverance that is similar to a biblical story of deliverance.

8
DEMONS

Demons are wicked, but thanks be to God, they're completely defeated because of the victory of the cross by Jesus Christ. Christ gave us authority over demons.

BEHOLD, I GIVE UNTO YOU POWER TO TREAD ON SERPENTS AND SCORPIONS, AND OVER ALL THE POWER OF THE ENEMY: AND NOTHING SHALL BY ANY MEANS HURT YOU.

(LUKE 10:19)

I've ministered to thousands of people who've felt something leave them when I've addressed a particular spirit. Most people don't even realize they're being oppressed until the oppression has lifted. The resulting sensation is usually a feeling of lightness.

The enemy weighs people down slowly so that they

don't recognize it happening. Feeling light is synonymous to being set free from a burden. The feeling of being oppressed is a heavy burden.

Countless people walk through life being burdened in a way that's unnecessary, but since they refuse to come to Christ, the burden continues and gets heavier.

FOR MY YOKE IS EASY,

AND MY BURDEN IS LIGHT.

(MATTHEW 11:30)

I've seen a number of demons, but usually when ministering I see the effect of a demon rather than actually seeing a demon. It becomes easy to discern what's happening to a person if you've had enough practice speaking to people.

Discernment is exercised by getting involved in conversation with a variety of people in the marketplace. Just as it can become easy to see Christ in people by recognizing the peace on them, it can become easy to see the oppression of the enemy on them.

Ahava and I were recently driving somewhere and we passed a young man and woman selling stuff on the lot of an old, abandoned gas station. As we drove past I could see the oppression on them invited by disobedience. I sensed the disobedience was from drugs, alcohol and rage.

You may be thinking why we didn't stop to talk to them. I didn't lack compassion for them, but rather discerned that the Spirit wasn't moving me to stop and talk with them.

Jesus wants to save them, but he also has a time for dealing with people. Jesus will often wait until people humble themselves before he brings his servants across their path.

BUT HE GIVETH MORE GRACE. WHEREFORE HE SAITH,

GOD RESISTETH THE PROUD, BUT GIVETH GRACE UNTO THE HUMBLE.

(JAMES 4: 6)

Humility is the key to abiding in the peace of the Lord. Humility is defined by walking in love and not thinking too highly of yourself. That young couple needed deliverance from a number of demons. We did pray for them while driving after we passed them and I'm sure that prayer activated the work of the Lord in their lives to bring about a willingness to listen to the counsel of the Lord.

TO OPEN THEIR EYES, AND TO TURN THEM FROM DARKNESS TO LIGHT, AND FROM THE POWER OF SATAN UNTO GOD,

THAT THEY MAY RECEIVE FORGIVENESS OF SINS, AND INHERITANCE AMONG THEM WHICH ARE SANCTIFIED BY FAITH THAT IS IN ME.

(ACTS 26:18)

Sin isn't the only thing that opens a spiritual door for a person to be attacked and oppressed by a demon. Sometimes a person has a demon because of ignorance or when they were young a parent opened a spiritual door of attack, which makes them a victim.

Such was the case with a woman I met at a church meeting in England. This story makes the point of sometimes needing to specifically identify a demon in order to cast it out. This lady's hand was closed in a fist for 32 years. I pried her fingers open and straightened them out completely, but when I let go they snapped back closed like a mouse trap being sprung.

She said, "I have really bad arthritis and have had many people pray for me over the years, but nothing has ever changed." I replied, "That's not arthritis. It's a demon."

She gasped in shock as she covered her mouth. I told

her not be afraid and then asked her if her mom was into witchcraft. “Yes, she was! How did you know?” she replied stunned.

I discerned that her mom had opened a door to the demonic by entertaining witchcraft through mediums and tarot cards. The demon latched onto this lady and kept her hand closed in a fist for 32 years.

For about 10 minutes I tapped her hand and told the spirits of witchcraft and sorcery to get out and for the first time in 32 years she was freely opening and closing her hand. Two weeks later I spoke with a good friend, Rob Taylor and he told me that she’s still free and getting baptized next week. Praise the Lord!

All the people that prayed for her over the years were incorrectly addressing the situation. It wasn't arthritis. The attack was a demon from witchcraft and sorcery.

The point is clear that sometimes you have to address what’s happening in a very specific way. This speaks of the need to hear from the Lord and obey instructions, rather than simply repeating generalized command statements of healing.

That situation is similar to an account in the bible, in terms of the length of time being oppressed by the enemy.

AND, BEHOLD, THERE WAS A WOMAN WHICH HAD A SPIRIT OF INFIRMITY EIGHTEEN YEARS, AND WAS BOWED TOGETHER, AND COULD IN NO WISE LIFT UP HERSELF.

AND WHEN JESUS SAW HER, HE CALLED HER TO HIM, AND SAID UNTO HER, WOMAN, THOU ART LOOSED FROM THINE INFIRMITY.

AND HE LAID HIS HANDS ON HER: AND IMMEDIATELY SHE WAS MADE STRAIGHT, AND GLORIFIED GOD.

(LUKE 13:11-13)

Ahava and I were ministering in a house church in Detroit. We met a young woman who was very pleasant and seemed quite normal as we engaged in conversation with her before the meeting.

During the meeting we went around the room laying hands on people and when we came to her and laid hands on her, she started to scream and writhe like a snake as she began sliding off the chair to the floor.

We felt compelled to command the spirit of death out of her and later discovered that she had a number of miscarriages and was even in the midst of having another one.

After being delivered, she was very peaceful. People can look fine on the outside, but on the inside all sorts of horrible things can be happening.

AND THEY BROUGHT HIM UNTO HIM: AND WHEN HE SAW HIM, STRAIGHTWAY THE SPIRIT TARE HIM; AND HE FELL ON THE GROUND, AND WALLOWED FOAMING.

(MARK 9:20)

One night while sleeping, I was attacked by a demon. Something was bouncing me on my bed and also keeping me from speaking. When I was finally able to call out to Jesus, I thought it would stop but it didn't, which made me a bit nervous.

However, I recognized that I now had the strength to resist this attack. I pushed myself up from the bed and when I turned around, there in my bedroom stood a demon in the form of a man.

He had some sort of mechanical device in his hands, which I surmised was what he was using to attack me. When I saw him, he was frozen in place because the victory was already mine. I took two steps towards him, grabbed him by the neck and started to smash him on the ground before throwing him out of my home through the wall. Then I went back to sleep and slept more peacefully than I'd ever slept before. I knew why I slept so peacefully. I just gained revelation of my authority over the enemy. I already knew I had authority, but now it was experiential.

For this reason, I don't have a problem with demonic attacks. I always win and gain experiential knowledge of my authority over the enemy's attacks.

About a year later, while sleeping, I was attacked by a demon that was paralyzing me so that I couldn't speak or move my body. However, I was able to move my head and when I lifted my head to look towards the end of the bed, there stood a figure in a creepy, black, flowing robe. I turned my head to my left. Ahava was beside me sleeping soundly. I looked back at this demon and because it was preventing me from speaking, I thought in my mind, "As soon as I get up from here, I'm gonna wring your neck."

Immediately, I was free and it was gone. I thought to myself, "He must have heard the news of what I did to that other fellow."

It doesn't end there. Recently Ahava came under attack from the enemy. She was at home in North Carolina and I was up north. I called her because she had mentioned in an email that she was in pain. When she answered the phone, she sounded rigid. She had a lot of pain in her back and when she moved a certain way or took a deep breath, the pain was almost unbearable.

I commanded the pain to leave in the name of Jesus and some of it left. Then it came to my remembrance about the demon whose neck I wrung and so I began to say, "If you don't let go of my wife, I am going to come there in the spirit and wring your neck!" Immediately she was free.

Either it was the same demon I defeated in the past, or it was a demon who heard the news about what I'd done.

AND IT CAME TO PASS, WHEN THEY BROUGHT OUT THOSE KINGS UNTO JOSHUA,

THAT JOSHUA CALLED FOR ALL THE MEN OF ISRAEL, AND SAID UNTO THE CAPTAINS OF THE MEN OF WAR WHICH WENT WITH HIM,

COME NEAR, PUT YOUR FEET UPON THE NECKS OF THESE KINGS. AND THEY CAME NEAR, AND PUT THEIR FEET UPON THE NECKS OF THEM.

AND JOSHUA SAID UNTO THEM,

FEAR NOT, NOR BE DISMAYED, BE STRONG AND OF GOOD COURAGE:

FOR THUS SHALL THE LORD DO TO ALL YOUR ENEMIES AGAINST WHOM YE FIGHT.

(JOSHUA 10:24-25)

If you are a born-again Christian, this word is for you as well. You will wring the necks of these defeated demons, so don't be afraid or timid. Be bold and mighty in the Lord. Jesus is Lord!

Earlier in this chapter I mentioned witchcraft and sorcery. Witchcraft is rebellion against the Lord. It's trying to gain influence in the spirit realm in order to achieve a desired result in the natural realm, but doing so in a way that the Lord doesn't approve of.

FOR REBELLION IS AS THE SIN OF WITCHCRAFT,

AND STUBBORNNESS IS AS INIQUITY AND IDOLATRY.

BECAUSE THOU HAST REJECTED THE WORD OF THE LORD,

HE HATH ALSO REJECTED THEE FROM BEING KING.

(1SAMUEL 15:23)

The only spiritually legal way of doing anything is through Jesus Christ and according to His word. This is called obedience.

In the scripture verse I just highlighted, (1Samuel 15:23) the prophet Samuel rebuked King Saul because Saul disobeyed the command of the Lord.

He was told to destroy the wicked Amalekites and all their possessions. Instead, Saul kept the cattle in order to sacrifice them to the Lord. He thought he was doing a good thing by sacrificing to the Lord with those animals. This is the spiritual equivalent of people doing their own good works and believing those works are pleasing to the Lord.

It's important to bring people to repentance once they're free from oppression. If they don't repent of and renounce the behavior that brought the demon in the first place, the demon will come back and oftentimes with a vengeance.

9

DREAMS AND VISIONS

I've had dreams and visions that will help you to recognize how ministry is supernatural and not something that is accomplished on your own strength.

AND THE LORD ANSWERED ME: "WRITE THE VISION; MAKE IT PLAIN ON TABLETS, SO HE MAY RUN WHO READS IT."

(HABAKKUK 2:2)

Dreams and visions are from the Lord. They're often mysterious and hard to understand, but the Spirit reveals mysteries. I've often said that Christianity is the ministry of the Spirit.

It's important to realize this truth in order for the Lord to effectively use you to set captives free in ministry situations.

HOWEVER, THERE IS A GOD IN HEAVEN WHO REVEALS MYSTERIES ...

(DANIEL 2:28)

A number of years ago I was on a plane and there were two women sitting to my right. They knew I was a minister because I told them. When flying, I will either have conversation with the people next to me, or close my eyes, or read something, or listen to music on my phone.

The women were a mother and daughter travelling together. The mother was right next to me. I don't remember how the conversation led to this, but the mother mentioned how her husband was deceased and she wasn't sure how he felt about her at the end of his life because their relationship was not good at that time.

After she told me this and we had some more conversation, I decided to close my eyes to relax or possibly fall asleep.

All of a sudden a man appears before me in the spirit. He looked like Jerry Garcia, who used to be the lead singer and guitar player for the Grateful Dead. I kept my eyes closed looking at him and realized he was alive and not just a picture. I knew this was the husband. In my mind, I spoke to him. I asked, "Are you the husband?" He nodded his head yes. Then I asked him, "Are you mad at her?" He shook his head no. He disappeared and I opened my eyes in total amazement.

I turn my head to the right and asked them, "Did he look like Jerry Garcia?" Their eyes bulged and their mouths dropped open. Immediately, the daughter got her tablet out and showed me pictures of her dad. He looks like Jerry Garcia.

Also, in this vision, the man was wearing sunglasses similar to the type Jerry Garcia would wear at times. She showed me pictures of her dad wearing similar sunglasses. I told them what happened and what I had asked him in the spirit and how he responded and they were both shocked, but also very comforted. Then I told them I would try and get him to come back, as I closed my eyes.

Remarkably he started to reappear, but I couldn't hold him. He faded away. It's important to note that the Spirit allowed this to happen for me for the purpose of comforting them both, but it wasn't for me to try and make this happen on my own just because I was fascinated or wanted to know more.

Trying to do something like this without the Lord

doing it is rebellion.

A good example of this rebellion is found in another experience I had in which I invited the attack of demons because of my rebellion. One night while lying in bed before falling asleep, I decided I would try to look into the spirit realm to open a portal.

Surprisingly enough, I did!

With my eyes closed, I saw a portal open up. It started as a small circle and quickly opened wide. Soon after, a pack of about 6 black dogs came through the portal and started playing with each other. These dogs were all identical and looked like older puppies of about 6 to 8 months. I was being entertained by what I was seeing.

However, soon enough something came through the portal that seemed a bit disturbing because I didn't recognize it as a dog or any other creature on earth. Then another disturbing creature came through! Then more and more grotesque things started flooding through this portal!

This was very disturbing and incredible because things were coming through so fast that I couldn't recognize them as they were coming through. It was like a blur when something goes past you real quick. All of a sudden I started to feel things moving under my comforter!

This scared me and I quickly called out, "Angels come now!"

Immediately I saw 3 or 4 flashes of light, like lightening bolts, come from above the portal. Everything went back into the portal and it closed. Wow! Needless to say, I repented and have never tried that again.

One night I had a dream in which I found myself on the stone driveway of a house on the beach. The front of the house faced the beach and was right on the beach. The back of the house had two attached garages. Both these garages were like bays of an auto mechanic shop. Jesus was the owner of the house. It was dusk.

All of a sudden I'm in one of the bays fixing a car. I took a part off the shelf and put it on the car and the car was fixed. I knew exactly where the part was to be found and how to fix the car.

Next, I'm back out on the driveway and it's morning. Jesus, from the kitchen window, asks me if I would like to see what I did to fix the car and naturally I said yes. I then see a picture of a pivoting auto part that reminded me of a part that would go on the front end of a vehicle for stability.

At this point Jesus gets into a blue van and drives down the road and stops about a quarter mile away for a cup of coffee.

I stood there wondering why he did this. Then I hear commotion in the front yard. I go around front and onto the beach. There are a number of people playing volleyball or something. There's also a cute puppy dog. I pick up the puppy and he begins to cry, so I put him down and go back around to the back of the house.

When I get there I hear noise in the garages. I go inside and see a man dressed in an outfit that makes him look like a parts repair and delivery man. We make eye contact and I nod at him and then begin to look at parts that I believe he'd just put down. I pick up one tool which I was interested in. It was a pair of hand shears that were just sharpened.

After I woke up I immediately received some revelation of the dream, but months later received a deeper revelation after having an experience in the natural that fit the dream.

The crying puppy dog represented the need for me to be gentle with people. The Lord was the parts delivery man and I was more interested in the tools he had given me rather than Him. That hurt, but I'm glad it was revealed to me.

Sometime later Ahava and I were in Scotland with Tim and Maria Curwen and their children. Tim is a pilot. One day he was compelled to watch street healing videos on YouTube and came across my video called, MUST WATCH DRAMATIC NEW YORK HEALING AND SALVATION. This video is on the playlist. As he is watching, he gets convicted in his heart of his need and gets saved. Praise the Lord! Tim tells this testimony in the Foreword of this book. He contacted me and we've been friends ever since.

While we were in Scotland visiting the Curwens, they invited a nephew over the house because this child was born with club feet. He's an incredibly sweet kid. We ministered to him and the Lord immediately begins to heal him. He wore braces on his legs for 7+ years. He took them off and started walking around and saying, "Almost perfect" in a very cute way.

Up to that point he had 4 surgeries and another one was scheduled. After seeing the surgeon the scheduled surgery was cancelled. At school he ran a race with his peers and won. The Curwen's home is near the beach. We went there and I baptized this child and the whole family, including Maria's mom Victoria. It was a lot of fun.

Do you see the comparison between the dream and what was to take place months later?

FOR THE LORD GOD DOES NOTHING WITHOUT REVEALING HIS SECRET TO HIS SERVANTS THE PROPHETS.

(AMOS 3:7)

I usually label dreams and visions as encounters because that's what they seem like. They've been so real, I feel like I was actually there or actually met the person who was in the dream or vision. I've had two encounters in dreams that make a good argument for the role of saints with Christ being actively involved in our lives on earth.

The book of Hebrews mentions the cloud of witnesses in Hebrews 12:1. The word, "witness" refers to believers because it's the same word used by Jesus in Acts 1:8 referring to his people who are to receive the Holy Spirit. Both times the word being used is, "martus", which when translated is the word "witness".

BUT YE SHALL RECEIVE POWER, AFTER THAT THE HOLY GHOST IS COME UPON YOU: AND YE SHALL BE WITNESSES UNTO ME BOTH IN JERUSALEM, AND IN ALL JUDAEA, AND IN SAMARIA, AND UNTO THE

UTTERMOST PART OF THE EARTH.

(ACTS 1:8)

WHEREFORE SEEING WE ALSO ARE COMPASSED ABOUT WITH SO GREAT A CLOUD OF WITNESSES,

LET US LAY ASIDE EVERY WEIGHT, AND THE SIN WHICH DOTH SO EASILY BESET US, AND LET US RUN WITH PATIENCE THE RACE THAT IS SET BEFORE US,

(HEBREWS 12:1)

The reason why I believe saints with Christ are actively involved in the ministries of believers on earth is because of what is mentioned at the end of Hebrews 11 concerning these witnesses.

Hebrews 11 is commonly referred to as the Hall of Faith, which is a play on the words, "Hall of Fame". The chapter shares with the reader the faithful lives of many bible figures and verses 39 and 40 say something amazing.

AND THESE ALL, HAVING OBTAINED A GOOD REPORT THROUGH FAITH,

RECEIVED NOT THE PROMISE:

GOD HAVING PROVIDED SOME BETTER THING FOR US,

THAT THEY WITHOUT US SHOULD NOT BE MADE PERFECT.

(HEBREWS 11:39-40)

Do you see the point I'm making? This cloud of witnesses are involved with us in order to complete what the Lord gave them to do.

Wow! This is the perspective I believe and my experiences back up this line of thinking. As I said earlier, I don't develop doctrine based on my experience. I develop doctrine through proper exegesis and rightly dividing the word and then my experience helps me to see that this is a correct view of God's word.

Now I will share the two dream encounters I had.

One night while asleep a man comes through a spiritual door and into my spiritual space. This didn't happen in the natural realm. It was during a dream/encounter. I knew immediately that this was TL Osborne. He didn't say anything. He just came through this door and had a big grin on his face.

One of the things that's interesting about this encounter is that I'd only seen perhaps 5 minutes of video on TL Osborne some 12-15 years earlier. I never studied his ministry, yet I knew this was him. If you've had experiences similar to this in the dream state, you know there's information in dreams that you just know. We don't know why we know things, but we do.

There's a scripture that alludes to knowing things without having studied.

FOR NOW WE SEE THROUGH A GLASS, DARKLY;

BUT THEN FACE TO FACE:

NOW I KNOW IN PART;

BUT THEN SHALL I KNOW EVEN AS ALSO I AM KNOWN.

(1CORINTHIANS 13:12)

I went onto YouTube to look for some TL Osborne videos and found plenty of them. TL is an amazing minister who, when in time, saw thousands of incredible miracles. In the videos I watched, he often had a big grin on his face. He was always happy with the joy of the Lord.

I was amazed watching videos with him because he came to me in the spirit. He's in the cloud of witnesses helping me and others. I have learned a lot from watching his videos.

The second dream I had that's similar involved another saint who's with the Lord. The man's name is Thomas Henderson and he was alive in America during the American Revolution. In the dream I saw a worn canvas bag. I opened the bag and there was a folded up garment. I unfolded the garment a little while it was in the canvas bag and I saw the name LT Thomas Henderson written on the garment.

When I woke up I did a search for him on the internet and discovered that he was an acting governor and was in the militia and the minutemen.

Here's a definition of minutemen.

MINUTEMEN WERE CIVILIAN COLONISTS WHO INDEPENDENTLY ORGANIZED TO FORM WELL- PREPARED MILITIA COMPANIES SELF-TRAINED IN WEAPONRY, TACTICS AND MILITARY STRATEGIES FROM THE AMERICAN COLONIAL PARTISAN MILITIA DURING

THE AMERICAN REVOLUTIONARY WAR.

THEY WERE ALSO KNOWN FOR BEING READY IN A MINUTE'S NOTICE.

THEY PROVIDED A HIGHLY MOBILE, RAPIDLY DEPLOYED FORCE THAT ALLOWED THE COLONIES TO RESPOND IMMEDIATELY TO WAR THREATS, HENCE THE NAME.

I find this totally fascinating because it brings to mind scripture that speaks of our need to be ready at all times because we're in a spiritual war and the enemy is always on the prowl.

PUT ON THE WHOLE ARMOUR OF GOD, THAT YE MAY BE ABLE TO STAND AGAINST THE WILES OF THE DEVIL.

(EPHESIANS 6:11)

BE SOBER, BE VIGILANT; BECAUSE YOUR ADVERSARY THE DEVIL, AS A ROARING LION, WALKETH ABOUT, SEEKING WHOM HE MAY DEVOUR:

(1PETER 5:8)

PREACH THE WORD; BE INSTANT IN SEASON, OUT OF SEASON;

REPROVE, REBUKE, EXHORT WITH ALL LONG SUFFERING AND DOCTRINE.

(2TIMOTHY 4:2)

BUT SANCTIFY THE LORD GOD IN YOUR HEARTS: AND BE READY ALWAYS TO GIVE AN ANSWER

TO EVERY MAN THAT ASKETH YOU A REASON OF THE HOPE THAT IS IN YOU WITH MEEKNESS AND FEAR:

(1PETER 3:15)

What's really cool about this dream involving Lt Thomas Henderson is that he lived in Freehold, NJ, which is the town where I became a born-again Christian.

He was laid to rest in Old Tennent Cemetery. It just so happens that when I was in high school and running on the cross-country and track teams, we used to run through this cemetery regularly because it was convenient.

After having this experience, Ahava and I went to the cemetery and found his grave marker. It's in a spot nowhere near where we used to run some 35+ years earlier.

I believe this dream was about a spiritual mantle that's available to me if I take it. I'm not sure of the implications of this, but I'm certainly not fearful or concerned about the implications even if the mantle comes with great responsibility and/or persecution.

As I've said, I believe TL Osborne and Lt Thomas Henderson are in the cloud of witnesses and are involved in the ministries of certain believers and Hebrews 11:39-40 confirms this.

10
TIPS ON HOW TO MINISTER

Many believers who are interested in street ministry want to know how to approach people on the streets. I've always found it easy to approach people on the streets, but not everyone feels this is an easy thing to do. To be frank, there are no secrets or best approaches.

Many methods of approaching people work and if you ask the Lord, He will give you a method tailor made for you.

As I shared earlier, the Lord gave me a method of approach with the camera that worked immediately. You don't need to video record the ministry situations and that will make your approach easy. I've approached thousands of people and most of the situations are without the camera. The videos I've made are only a small percentage of all I've seen the Lord do in the marketplace.

There are many little clues that help you know who to approach.

What I look for the most is humility.

Humility can be seen on people. It comes across as a peaceful, soft look on their face and a walking posture that is somewhat naive-looking and carefree. Humility is not fearful and it's what the Lord highly esteems. The humble aren't afraid to engage you in conversation. It's easy to look them in the eyes because they're not afraid. They automatically give you their attention without suspicion.

In other words, they won't think you're out to get something from them. When you meet someone like this, it's easy to share the truth with them. You will walk away feeling good even if they're not ready to believe the message about Jesus. Check out the video on my playlist called, "Jewish man healed CLASSIC reaction", to see a person that I believe fits this description.

If I don't make my approach with a camera, I will say a number of different things because every situation is different. If someone is walking towards me and I'm interested in talking to this person, I will usually start talking to them from about 10 feet away. This immediately gets their attention as we are approaching each other and gives the person a chance to make a decision about me a good 5 or 6 feet away, which gives them a little buffer zone and makes them comfortable.

I rarely start talking as the person is passing me because this can be startling. The only time I do this is when I feel the power of God for the person as I'm passing. At this point I will turn around toward them and say something like, "Excuse me. Can I ask you something?" If I say this loud enough, they know I'm talking to them.

When I feel the power of God for someone, the response is always positive. When I speak with a total stranger, I maintain a posture that says I'm already a good friend with that person and that what I'm doing is perfectly normal. In other words, I don't doubt myself when I speak to someone.

Your posture is something that people recognize immediately. Your posture is defined as, the way you hold yourself, the way you walk, the way you talk, the level of rest in your face, the amount your eyes are opened, etc.

There are many clues that reveal to you if someone is approachable. The other day I was in Trader Joe's doing some grocery shopping. There was a woman on crutches walking towards me. I moved my cart out of her way and she smiled at my gesture of consideration. At once I knew she was approachable because of her thankful smile. I asked her how she hurt herself.

Not everyone who needs healing is displaying an outward sign that gives you a clue that they need healing, but this was obvious, so my approach was easy.

If you see someone who is clearly hurt, just ask them how they got hurt. They will gladly tell you.

When she was done telling me, I told her I'm a minister and that I pray for people and they get healed.

You can say the same thing when you meet people because every Christian is a minister. We're all called to the ministry of reconciliation to tell people that God has forgiven them through his Son Jesus.

By the way, the lady was healed. She had broken some toes and was in pain. I put my foot against her foot and the fire of God entered her.

She felt the fire and the throbbing pain went away.

TO WIT, THAT GOD WAS IN CHRIST, RECONCILING THE WORLD UNTO HIMSELF, NOT IMPUTING THEIR TRESPASSES UNTO THEM;

AND HATH COMMITTED UNTO US THE WORD OF RECONCILIATION.

NOW THEN WE ARE AMBASSADORS FOR CHRIST, AS THOUGH GOD DID BESEECH YOU BY US: WE PRAY YOU IN CHRIST'S STEAD, BE YE RECONCILED TO GOD.

(2CORINTHIANS 5:19-20)

The best way to make this point is through healing because the Lord links the forgiveness of sins together with healing. They are, in essence, the same thing. This is made perfectly clear in the account of the man sick of the palsy in the gospel of Matthew. The account is also told in Mark's gospel.

AND AGAIN HE ENTERED INTO CAPERNAUM AFTER SOME DAYS; AND IT WAS NOISED THAT HE WAS IN THE HOUSE.

AND STRAIGHTWAY MANY WERE GATHERED TOGETHER, INSOMUCH THAT

THERE WAS NO ROOM TO RECEIVE THEM, NO, NOT SO MUCH AS ABOUT THE DOOR:

AND HE PREACHED THE WORD UNTO THEM. AND THEY COME UNTO HIM, BRINGING ONE SICK OF THE PALSY, WHICH WAS BORNE OF FOUR. AND WHEN THEY COULD NOT COME NIGH UNTO HIM FOR THE PRESS,

THEY UNCOVERED THE ROOF WHERE HE WAS: AND WHEN THEY HAD BROKEN IT UP,

THEY LET DOWN THE BED WHEREIN THE SICK OF THE PALSY LAY.

WHEN JESUS SAW THEIR FAITH, HE SAID UNTO THE SICK OF THE PALSY, SON, THY SINS BE FORGIVEN THEE.

BUT THERE WAS CERTAIN OF THE SCRIBES SITTING THERE, AND REASONING IN THEIR HEARTS, WHY DOTH THIS MAN THUS SPEAK BLASPHEMIES?

WHO CAN FORGIVE SINS BUT GOD ONLY?

AND IMMEDIATELY WHEN JESUS PERCEIVED IN HIS SPIRIT THAT THEY SO REASONED WITHIN THEMSELVES, HE SAID UNTO THEM,

WHY REASON YE THESE THINGS IN YOUR HEARTS? WHETHER IS IT EASIER TO SAY TO THE SICK OF THE PALSY, THY SINS BE FORGIVEN THEE; OR TO SAY, ARISE, AND TAKE UP THY BED, AND WALK?

BUT THAT YE MAY KNOW THAT THE SON OF MAN HATH POWER ON EARTH TO FORGIVE SINS,

(HE SAITH TO THE SICK OF THE PALSY,) I SAY UNTO THEE, ARISE, AND TAKE UP THY BED, AND GO THY WAY INTO THINE HOUSE.

AND IMMEDIATELY HE AROSE, TOOK UP THE BED, AND WENT FORTH BEFORE THEM ALL;

INSOMUCH THAT THEY WERE ALL AMAZED, AND GLORIFIED GOD, SAYING, WE NEVER SAW IT ON THIS FASHION.

(MARK 2:1-12)

This isn't an invitation to tell everyone their sins are forgiven because many people harden their hearts and willfully go on in their sins.

This word is for the humble and those are the people I look for. They get healed the easiest. Jesus has atoned for the sins of the whole world, but this gift is only received through repentance. Faith in Jesus is a sign of repentance and so is humility.

When I'm talking with someone, I don't stare at them non-stop.

This is very uncomfortable for the person. I will look them in the eyes and then look away. I do this many times. This gives the person a chance to relax when I'm looking away. It also gives them a chance to check me out a bit closer so they can know for sure that I'm not a threat to them.

When I say something, I will usually watch for their reaction before turning away my eyes. A person's reaction shows up in their facial muscles and their eyes. How they react to what I say determines the next thing I will say. The back and forth conversation between me and someone I'm ministering to is really somewhat of a game. I'm trying to convince them of my belief system.

Even if they're already a believer, I may still be trying to convince them of my way of thinking because many believers have a perspective of God's word that I feel is inaccurate, especially if they don't experience the power of the Holy Spirit in their walk with Jesus.

I try to be agreeable as much as possible without compromising what the word of God says. If someone says something to me that may sound a bit off, I will still agree, but then share what I believe is a more accurate view.

It's important to slowly win people over to your way of thinking. Slowly and carefully because that's what works. If I say something that is radically different from their way of thinking, there's a chance I will be cut off and nothing else I say will be received.

There's a portion of scripture that makes this point.

AND HE SPAKE ALSO A PARABLE UNTO THEM;

NO MAN PUTTETH A PIECE OF A NEW GARMENT UPON AN OLD;

IF OTHERWISE, THEN BOTH THE NEW MAKETH A RENT, AND THE PIECE THAT WAS TAKEN OUT OF THE NEW AGREETH NOT WITH THE OLD.

AND NO MAN PUTTETH NEW WINE INTO OLD BOTTLES;

ELSE THE NEW WINE WILL BURST THE BOTTLES, AND BE SPILLED, AND THE BOTTLES SHALL PERISH.

BUT NEW WINE MUST BE PUT INTO NEW BOTTLES; AND BOTH ARE PRESERVED.

NO MAN ALSO HAVING DRUNK OLD WINE STRAIGHTWAY DESIRETH NEW:

FOR HE SAITH, THE OLD IS BETTER.

(LUKE 5:36-39)

People get accustomed to the way they think and very comfortable with their own biblical world view. People don't like change, so this is the main reason why ministry has to be supernatural. The supernatural gets the attention of people and they become more apt to listen to your view.

THEN SAID JESUS UNTO HIM, EXCEPT YE SEE SIGNS AND WONDERS, YE WILL NOT BELIEVE.

(JOHN4:48)

If you're born-again, you have the Spirit of God in you. This makes you able to minister in the supernatural.

My friend Doug Collins shared with me a good approach. He would say to people, "Would you be offended if I prayed for you?" I think this is brilliant because nobody wants to admit to being easily offended.

Doug is in Ontario Canada. He gets great results ministering healing in the marketplace and makes videos as well. His YouTube channel name is, "Windsor on Fire". Doug models some of his ministry after Tom Loud, who also gets great results ministering in the marketplace and has a Youtube channel after his name.

If you have a heart to help people and you're completely convinced of the message of reconciliation and the need to operate in the power of the Holy Spirit, you will find a way to approach people and carry on a conversation with them. If you're just starting out, don't be afraid. Leave the results to the Lord. By sharing the good news with people, you're being obedient. God is the healer, so just do your part in obedience and leave the results to the Lord.

If you're not seeing a lot of results, keep talking to

people because the more people you talk to, the better you will become at discerning who's ready to receive. The enemy messes with people so that they will reject truth, but you can become aware of Satan's schemes to mess with people and this will help you to know what to say to people.

BUT STRONG MEAT BELONGETH TO THEM THAT ARE OF FULL AGE,

EVEN THOSE WHO BY REASON OF USE HAVE THEIR SENSES EXERCISED TO DISCERN BOTH GOOD AND EVIL.

(HEBREWS 5:14)

Some people are ready to receive and others aren't. If someone isn't ready to receive, it doesn't mean the Lord doesn't want to heal them. It just means some thinking needs to change in order for them to receive. You can lead a horse to water, but you can't make him drink. Healing is a gift and you can't force someone to receive a gift. How often do people, out of pride, refuse a gift?

This happens a lot when it's time to pay a restaurant bill. One person will say, "I will get that!" and the other person might say, "No, that's not necessary." Something in people makes them have an immediate reaction of not wanting something for free. I've been guilty of this myself. I know where this thinking comes from. The enemy of our souls messes with our thinking if we're not diligent.

If you've seen enough of my healing videos, you've seen how I will ask the person I've just ministered to if anything has changed. If you're not seeing immediate results yet, don't ask the person if anything has changed. Take the posture that you don't need to hear them say, "Yes, I feel better". Let them offer that information to you.

This will cut down on you having to hear that the issue is the same. The truth is, the pain or sickness doesn't need to go away immediately. I've been in many situations where nothing happened immediately, but later on, or the next day, the person was healed. There's a very healthy effect of not asking the person if anything has changed after you minister, although I do it most of the time.

Simply ministering and not asking if anything has changed can help you to develop the attitude that they're healed regardless, because you prayed for them. You really don't need to hear them say they feel better. I do it because I'm making videos and I want to get the reaction on video for many people to see and hear, in order to teach with the videos.

If you carefully consider this, it's an accurate approach because it shows that you're leaning on the word by faith and not by sight.

AND THESE SIGNS SHALL FOLLOW THEM THAT BELIEVE;

IN MY NAME SHALL THEY CAST OUT DEVILS; THEY SHALL SPEAK WITH NEW TONGUES;

THEY SHALL TAKE UP SERPENTS; AND IF THEY DRINK ANY DEADLY THING, IT SHALL NOT HURT THEM;

THEY SHALL LAY HANDS ON THE SICK, AND THEY SHALL RECOVER.

(MARK 16:17-18)

I have a cool testimony of healing where I didn't inquire afterwards if the person was healed.

I was in a Home Depot store a number of years ago and I saw an employee walking with a cane. I said to him, "Hey, you're too young to be walking with a cane! What happened to you"? He gave me a simple reply that he hurt his back, which is fine because I was just starting a conversation and it didn't matter how many details he gave me. I told him I pray for people and they get healed instantly. I was in a hurry, so I prayed for him and then left.

Two years later I'm in the same store and there are 2 employees working behind the counter of the tool rental section. I get a word of knowledge that one of them has pain. He did have pain behind his left ear. I reached over and quickly laid my hand there for 2 seconds as I said a few words and he was instantly healed.

As soon as that happened, the employee standing right next to him says to me, "You know, you were in here a couple years ago and prayed for me because I hurt my back". I look at him and tried to remember, but couldn't. He told me a few more details, such as having to use a cane and then I remembered him.

He goes on to say, "You said when you pray for people they get healed instantly. Well, nothing happened and my co-workers laughed at that. However, the next day I woke up completely healed and they weren't laughing after that."

I had to wait 2 years to hear that testimony, but it was worth the wait.

When deciding on who to minister to, I will take into account the age difference between people who are in a group. A good example is a family. I rarely approach a family of mom, dad and young kids because mom and dad go into protection mode when a stranger approaches. Unfortunately, most people can't discern a real threat from that of a man of God bringing good news. This is from a lack of pursuing the Lord in his word and prayer. It's fear-based.

When approaching young people, I rarely approach a group larger than 4. This is because the enemy takes advantage of my inability to manage a large group without confusion. If there's a young person in the group with a mocking spirit, that spirit will notice this management issue and stir up the kid to be a disturbance.

When ministering to a group of youth and several have pain or sickness, I will minister first to the one that I deem is the most humble, since the humble get healed the easiest.

I rarely approach someone who is walking fast or is wearing headphones.

I rarely run after someone who has passed me by, but if I do, I make sure I call out to the person long before I get to him. It's usually fruitless to run after someone unless I felt the power of God for that person.

If someone gets healed, I try not to keep him or her too long because they usually need to get away in order to process what just happened. This being the case, I say as much as possible in the time I have with them. Ideally, I want them to not be spooked by supernatural healing and to stick around and listen to everything I would like to tell them.

If someone gets healed and I feel like they're tight on money, I like to sow into them because they need the help and because they're good soil to sow into. Someone who just got healed is good soil to sow into.

It irritates me when someone in a group speaks for everyone else and says nobody needs healing. It's usually a fruitless situation and I try to end it as soon as possible.

I find it difficult to minister in crowded areas. What seems to work best is, not too many people and not too little. A market area with a steady flow of casual people but not too busy.

If I'm growing out someone's leg, it's imperative to keep the person perfectly steady with hips totally back against the bench. Afterwards, it's important to have the person stand up and walk around, at which time, I'm asking if they feel more level and if the pain is gone. I call this a supernatural chiropractic adjustment because most of these situations aren't really a leg growing, but rather tight muscles loosening.

Growing out legs has received a great deal of resistance from an unbelieving world, so it's very important to be diligent to follow the details I've mentioned. This is usually the case. I've actually grown out legs while the person was standing up. There's a good video of this on my YouTube playlist. It's called, "Leg grows while standing up".

If I do a particular healing a lot, I will get proficient with that technique.

When I first began healing and caught on to the whole leg growing thing, I was doing it a lot and got to the point where I could grow out a leg over the phone by just thinking the leg to grow. If a lot of time passes before doing a leg growing miracle, I will sometimes need to speak to the situation as opposed to simply thinking the leg to grow. We get good at something when we practice it a lot.

11
CARDBOARD BOX CHURCH

Ahava and I attend a church in Concord, North Carolina called, Fire Church. It's an excellent church with seasoned leaders who know their faith and the word. The founder of the church is Michael Brown. He's a well- known Messianic Jewish believer with a popular Christian radio program. The head pastor is Keith Collins. He's an awesome preacher/teacher moving in the supernatural. Another couple in leadership are Josh and Tobi Peters. They're instrumental in the church's missions outreaches. All these leaders were involved in the leadership of the Brownsville Assembly of God in Pensacola, Florida, where an amazing revival happened in the mid-late 90's.

In the summer of 2016 Scott Nary, an awesome brother in the Lord who moves in the prophetic as well as healing, organized a conference with Pastor Keith. They asked Scott Lee to come and minister as well. Scott Lee gets very specific words of knowledge that he combines with the prophetic and healing to greatly encourage people.

The conference was called, "The Perfect Power And Love Conference". After Scott Lee spoke, I wanted to have a word with him because I felt compelled to tell him what the Lord had been saying to me. I told Scott that the Lord had been prompting me to go minister in downtown Charlotte, which is about 30 minutes away. I drove down there one day and turned onto Trade Street and thought it was a great place to minister.

When I mentioned Trade Street to Scott, he stopped me and said he needed to share a story with me. He goes on to tell me about a vision from the Lord. "Tom, about 4 years ago I had this vision where I saw cardboard and duct tape coming down from Heaven and then I was standing in the vision with a box cutter in my hand. I saw the cardboard coming together as a little church with stained glass and painted white on the inside. The Lord told me to make a door for him to enter."

Scott went on to say, "Tom, when you said Trade Street, the Lord told me you were going to be the one who did Cardboard Box Church." I was blown away by this because I immediately saw the potential for an excellent way to minister and make the point of bringing the church to the streets.

The purpose of the church is the building up of the body of Christ for the work of ministry. Ministry is for this lost world to know that Jesus Christ is Lord and Savior. Ministry is to show this lost world that the sons of God are being revealed in Christ with great glory. We are to put this truth on display and convince men of their need. There are a couple good scripture verses that make this point.

AND HE GAVE SOME, APOSTLES;

AND SOME, PROPHETS;

AND SOME, EVANGELISTS;

AND SOME, PASTORS AND TEACHERS;

FOR THE PERFECTING OF THE SAINTS, FOR THE WORK OF THE MINISTRY, FOR THE EDIFYING OF THE BODY OF CHRIST:

(EPHESIANS 4:11-12)

ALL SCRIPTURE IS GIVEN BY INSPIRATION OF GOD, AND IS PROFITABLE FOR DOCTRINE, FOR REPROOF, FOR CORRECTION,

FOR INSTRUCTION IN RIGHTEOUSNESS: THAT THE MAN OF GOD MAY BE PERFECT, THOROUGHLY FURNISHED UNTO ALL GOOD WORKS.

(2TIMOTHY 3:16-17)

Cardboard Box Church makes this point really well. We encourage as many people as possible to make their own Cardboard Box Church and use it as an attention getter out in the marketplace.

It is indeed an attention getter. People passing by smile when they see it. They agree it's a good and novel idea. When people go inside they feel the presence of the Lord and that's not surprising because the Lord told Scott Lee to make sure there was a doorway for him to enter.

We've set up Cardboard Box Church (CBC) out in the marketplace many times already and have found it easy to minister to people passing by because it takes the attention off them and puts it on CBC. This is because I will usually say to the person that we're trying to bring attention to CBC since it's a God idea.

We set up a little bluetooth speaker inside and play worship music to set the atmosphere. During those times when people are not passing by, we will listen to the music and worship the Lord and pray for the town, or simply talk to each other about various topics. As of my writing this, CBC has only been set up in Charlotte, NC.

At first Ahava and I would set up in empty lots that looked unused, but quickly discovered that this doesn't work because even if a lot looks unused, it's still watched by people who own or manage it.

Such was the case with the first place we set up. Some of the neighboring businesses didn't want our little cardboard box church around for whatever reason. This is foolish thinking because the Lord would surely have blessed those neighboring businesses.

CBC is not difficult to assemble.

I've made a video that shows the process. The video is called Cardboard Box Church and it's on the playlist. I've made a number of changes to the church since the beginning. I started out making it too big and realized it wasn't stable enough. The whole concept of CBC needs to be duplicatable so that others can put it together easily and without frustration.

As of my writing this, I have a plan to make more changes. I plan on getting double-wall cardboard that is 24" x 72". 13 pieces this size will make the church. A future video will display this, so watch out for it. Perhaps both the new size and the video describing it will be out by the time your reading this.

There's too many big, expensive church buildings out there with Christians sitting in the pews thinking obedience is reading their bible, going to church and paying their tithe. That's not obedience. That's part of becoming equipped.

Obedience is being a doer of the word.

CBC makes this point.

BUT BE YE DOERS OF THE WORD,

AND NOT HEARERS ONLY,

DECEIVING YOUR OWN SELVES.

(JAMES 1:22)

12
HOW I TRAIN BELIEVERS

When I first started training believers to minister on the streets, I would go out to the streets with a disciple and minister to as many people as possible. Over the years I've changed my approach to what I believe is more accurate discipleship.

Praying for people on the streets is just one aspect of discipleship. When discipling a believer, it's important for them to accurately learn about their identity in Christ. Identity in Christ encompasses so much more than what believers are customarily taught in church. It's more than just going to heaven when we die. It's believing that Jesus makes you just like himself.

After all, he lives in you and puts the old man to death.

I AM CRUCIFIED WITH CHRIST:

NEVERTHELESS I LIVE;

YET NOT I, BUT CHRIST LIVETH IN ME:

AND THE LIFE WHICH I NOW LIVE IN THE FLESH

I LIVE BY THE FAITH OF THE SON OF GOD, WHO LOVED ME, AND GAVE HIMSELF FOR ME.

(GALATIANS 2:20)

Jesus empowers us to do what he did. To the extent that I believe that, I am able to help someone else get to that point.

THEN SAID JESUS TO THEM AGAIN, PEACE BE UNTO YOU: AS MY FATHER HATH SENT ME, EVEN SO SEND I YOU.

(JOHN 20:21)

Everyone that has a desire to operate in the supernatural power of the Holy Spirit can do so, if they have the Spirit of God in them. Believers I've discipled have grown into who they are in Christ and now they get results healing the sick.

Many of these believers have also learned from others, which is common. Nobody learns from just one teacher, but it's important to not have too many teachers because this breeds confusion. Confusion will frustrate your results in ministry because confusion breeds doubt.

BUT LET HIM ASK IN FAITH, NOTHING WAVERING.

FOR HE THAT WAVERETH IS LIKE A WAVE OF THE SEA DRIVEN WITH THE WIND AND TOSSED.

(JAMES 1:6)

When I train someone in the supernatural, I spend time with that person. We have many conversations together. We have meals together throughout the time we're with each other. We go into the marketplace to see what the Lord has for us to do. This is the model that brings believers to the place of understanding identity and moving in the supernatural.

Whatever is in me rubs off on the disciple and that only happens with spending time together and not just showing them how to pray for a few people on the streets. This is what Jesus did. He spent time with his disciples.

I've heard a few testimonies of believers saying that they started getting results healing the sick after spending time with another minister who gets results, but after awhile they stopped getting results.

The answer to this is clear. If you go on the streets with someone who gets results ministering healing and then you start to get results as well, it's most likely because of the belief of the one doing the discipling.

The disciple has to go home and make this his own. He has to take ownership of this and this only happens if the proper perspective is taught. I have a testimony that makes this point.

In 1997 I was attending a church in Virginia. The church leadership had just returned from the Brownsville Revival in Pensacola, Florida. This particular outpouring from God in Florida was the real deal and helped many people get right with God.

During the Sunday morning service after they returned from the revival, they were walking through the sanctuary laying hands on everyone. One of the leaders laid his hand on my head and spoke a few words including some scripture from Isaiah. I didn't think much of it, but I do remember the scripture.

TO OPEN THE BLIND EYES,

TO BRING OUT THE PRISONERS FROM THE PRISON,

AND THEM THAT SIT IN DARKNESS OUT OF THE PRISON HOUSE.

(ISAIAH 42:7)

As far as I recall, it was the very next day that I found myself praying for people and they were getting healed. This was the first time I ever did this. I hadn't studied healing scripture up to that point. I wasn't asking God to use me in healing. It just started happening.

This went on for several months, but then the power faded away. Or, more accurately, I faded away.

The point I'm making is that I was operating on an impartation that I didn't make my own. I didn't study healing scriptures. I didn't seek the counsel of other healers. I didn't do much of anything to turn this into a ministry of my own.

If you've been positively effected by the ministry the Lord has given me and would like 3 days of training, you can contact me. It's important for you to know that I don't diminish the value of what I have to offer.

That would cheapen God's power. You would need to provide travel and meal expenses. It would be very much appreciated if you shared a love offering for my time since this is what I do for a living. I earn my living from the gospel, which is biblical.

Our time together will be like the old saying, one hand washes another. We help each other. What we both get is priceless. I get the eternal reward of knowing that I've helped a new friend and brother in the Lord. Believers who go to church support the church with their finances because that's the proper order of things.

This is no different. I've found that those who understand this get the most out of training and are always blessed by the Lord.

BUT THIS I SAY, HE WHICH SOWETH SPARINGLY SHALL REAP ALSO SPARINGLY;

AND HE WHICH SOWETH BOUNTIFULLY SHALL REAP ALSO BOUNTIFULLY.

(2CORINTHIANS 9:6)

This method of training is much better than a conference with many attendees because conferences are not personal enough, but spending 3 days together with someone who operates in healing works wonders.

You can't get to know the leaders who run the conference, but you and I will know each other after our time together. I don't do this every month, so prayerfully consider if you want to do this, as I too will be in prayer about anyone who is interested.

Although I believe this method of training is more effective then conferences, I still believe conferences are effective. I have on my mind to do one day healing conferences with just Ahava and I teaching and ministering. There are many believers who just need a bit of sharpening and this would be effective for them in this regard.

God bless you for your time and support. I wouldn't have a ministry if the Lord didn't give me one. I'm very grateful to our Lord and to you.

EPILOGUE

Although this book has been mostly about my experiences with the power of the Holy Spirit out in the marketplace, the point of all this information is for the purpose of lost people being found.

If you don't know Jesus Christ in a personal way, I encourage you to believe in Him. Jesus came and taught us how to love and He taught us about His Father's kingdom. He was crucified and died for you. He shed his blood for you to be healed and forgiven.

AND ALMOST ALL THINGS ARE BY THE LAW PURGED WITH BLOOD; AND WITHOUT SHEDDING OF BLOOD IS NO REMISSION.

(HEBREWS 9:22)

Jesus loves you and wants you saved.

Please give your life to Jesus.

He will lead you and guide you all the days of your life.

He will never fail you nor abandon you.

You will have trials, but they come to make you a stronger person in Him. The rewards of knowing Jesus are incredible. If you walk with Him according to His word, the bible, you will overcome this world and enjoy great peace regardless of your circumstances.

Jesus will make you into the person you were meant to be and you will love the end result. Ask Him to reveal Himself to you, to forgive you of your sins and save you. God bless you.

Thomas Fischer

TOM FISCHER led the *Manalapan Braves* to a third place finish in the Meet of Champions cross country meet at Holmdel Park by placing seventh in the state individually.

I was a runner in school. We need to finish the race strong.

Five minutes earlier he was limping on his ankle.

When he took that stick in his hand, sickness left him. He was confused and kept looking at the stick.

I smiled at him the way Jesus would and life came back into his dead finger.

He was shocked when all the pain left immediately.

This pastor was healed when I put my shadow on his knee.

My beautiful wife Ahava & I in Galilee, Israel.

A still shot of my most popular video -
"MUST WATCH Dramatic New York Healing."

This is from the dramatic New York healing video. He was healed of a detached kneecap and tested it with a backflip.

From the streets of Lancaster, Pennsylvania. We meet a young Jewish woman who got healed and saved.

He said he felt like he was dipped in some sort of miracle oil.

This truck crossed at the moment I finished praying for this young man. It was divine timing.

YOUTUBE

www.youtube.com/user/mrtomff7

TOM FISCHER MINISTRIES

www.streethealing.com

tomfischerministries@gmail.com

CARDBOARD BOX CHURCH

cardboardboxchurch@gmail.com

www.cardboardboxchurch.com

23636807R00107

Printed in Great Britain
by Amazon